Prais

MW01487571

"A beautiful and blessed blend of contemporary real life and age-old Scripture, *Real Life with Mary* invites modern-day women to get to know our Blessed Mother not as a character from a story, but as a true friend, an inspiration, and a gift from the Father. Kelsey Gillespy shares her heart in these pages, and like Mary, she uses each word to direct attention not to herself, but to Christ. With prayer, reflection, contemplation, and action, each chapter is a mini-retreat. Taken together, this is a book sure to encourage women and so lift up their families for the glory of God."

— Lindsay Schlegel, author of *Don't Forget to Say Thank You: And Other Parenting Lessons That Brought Me Closer to God*

"Join Kelsey Gillespy in contemplating our Lady's virtues through everyday life, and discover that imitating them may not be as difficult as you think!"

— Amy Rodriguez, illustrator and digital artist

"Kelsey Gillespy, author of *In the Trenches: Finding God Through Parenting Littles*, has done it again—and, if possible, even better! *Real Life with Mary* is exquisite in every way: the conversational, accessible, sincere tone; the correlation of Mary's life with our own; the lovely prayers. I would recommend *Real Life with Mary* to anyone."

—Sister Mary Lea Hill, FSP, Crabby Mystic and author of
Growing in Virtue, One Vice at a Time

Real Life with MARY

GROWING IN VIRTUE TO MAGNIFY THE LORD

Kelsey Gillespy

Pauline
BOOKS & MEDIA
BOSTON

Library of Congress Control Number: 2023948856

ISBN 10: 0-8198-3174-3

ISBN 13: 978-0-8198-3174-3

Cover design by Tisa Muico

Published by Pauline Books & Media, 50 Saint Pauls Avenue, Boston, MA 02130-3491

Printed in the U.S.A.

www.pauline.org

Pauline Books & Media is the publishing house of the Daughters of St. Paul, an international congregation of women religious serving the Church with the communications media.

1 2 3 4 5 6 7 8 9   29 28 27 26 25 24

To Mary—
This is my attempt to paint your portrait in words.
It's more of a stick-figure scribbled in crayon,
but I offer it to you as a gift of love, nonetheless.

To my girls—
May you always know what it means to be a virtuous woman
because you've followed the lead of our beautiful Mother
and have become one yourselves.

Contents

INTRODUCTION

There's Something about Mary

I met my husband on a long-distance blind date.

He was a cute, Catholic-raised boy with a life and steady job halfway across the country. I, on the other hand, was floundering about in my faith, finishing up my undergrad degree and moving forward toward a future that was *not* halfway across the country.

There he was, so solid in his Catholic faith, living it out in such a beautiful, magnetic way. And there I was, groping through life, thirsting to learn more about Jesus, but feeling forever parched. How was a woman in the twenty-first century supposed to live like Christ?

I understood how to pursue the world, no doubt. I knew how to set goals and achieve them. But doing that while living like Jesus? I had no idea how to do that. I didn't even know what "living like Jesus" meant. Was I supposed to walk around performing miracles? Forgiving people? Loving people? What did it even mean to love people like Jesus?

When the weekends came, my cute boyfriend and I spent every Saturday night together at Catholic Mass and every Sunday morning at random Protestant churches, shopping to find one that fit. We tried big Bible churches. Non-denominational churches. Old churches. New churches. None of them hit the spot. None of them answered the questions that burned so deeply within my heart: How can I live like Christ right here, right now? What does a God-loving, virtuous woman look like today?

The searching and shuttling back and forth to various churches all weekend, every weekend was not only disappointing, it was also flat-out exhausting. We were both feeling it. One night, as we hung out on the couch watching TV, that handsome, Christ-like boyfriend of mine nonchalantly turned and looked me square in the eyes. "When we're married, I'd like us to be the same denomination."

The words sucked all the air out of the room.

Was I supposed to focus on the marriage part of his sentence? Or the same denomination part? Up until that point, we hadn't discussed either one. Surprisingly, I was cool with the marriage part. I knew I loved this boy more than anything else in the world. There was no doubt that I wanted to spend the rest of my life with him.

But the same denomination thing? I mean, this guy had been Catholic since birth, while I still bounced around from church to church, struggling to understand Jesus. It was clear which one of us would be changing.

I was livid. Enraged. Hurt. Confused. After all, I was trying so hard to get my Christian legs beneath me, and now I was being asked to uproot and plant myself somewhere else? *And* get married? It was all too much.

Once I cooled off, I realized if I was truly seeking Christ, why *not* check into Catholicism? Shouldn't I exhaust every possible avenue until I found him?

And so I began. At first, I treaded lightly, cautiously tip-toeing each step of the way through Catholic doctrine. But the more I looked, the more I learned; the more I learned, the more I fell head-over-heels in love with Christ. My quest for Truth—my quest for Christ— had crash-landed me into his one, true Church. Slowly but surely, I stopped perceiving Jesus as some obscure being that was too distant to grasp and started to understand him as a real, physical Person. One I could literally hold in the palm of my hand.

I quickly realized I wasn't *changing* my faith. Nor was I being uprooted and planted somewhere else. Quite the opposite, in fact. Now, with the richness of Catholic teaching to guide me, my Christian roots dug deeper and stronger than ever before. And, as my sweet, Christlike boyfriend predicted, I got confirmed in the Church one month before we got married.

Boy, did that open a whole can of worms. Now, I was Catholic. I was married. And, soon, I was pregnant. And I had no clue how to be any of those things.

Merely months before, I had been surging through life, slaying goals and pushing toward promising careers as a journalist and high school basketball coach—both of which had been front and center of the dream life I envisioned. Now I had to think about others? Put them *first*, even, and sacrifice myself?

This was nothing like what I had planned. Instead of conquering the world, I was now drowning in seas of confusion and desperation, cluelessly fumbling through my life as a Catholic woman, wife, and mother. Over time, one baby turned into two, then three, then four, and five. Finally—*finally*—I did something utterly Catholic. I took a closer look at Mary.

Up until that point, I'd thought Mary was a passive, goody-two-shoes type, flat and unrelatable. I mean, she was perfect and her kid was perfect. How hard could life be for someone like that? That kind of character didn't seem realistic, let alone intriguing, so I glossed over the verses in Scripture that mentioned her name.

Yeah, yeah, Mary said yes to the angel Gabriel.

Yeah, yeah, she helped her cousin.

Yeah, yeah, she gave birth to Jesus.

But when I started to *really* look at Scripture—to examine it, gnaw on it, and ponder it as Mary did—I found someone altogether different.

I found someone who said yes to Jesus before he even manifested himself in human form. Someone who was so in love with God, she would do anything for him, including tarnish her reputation and risk her life. Someone who, by her very nature of being filled with grace, must have had a difficult time fitting in with the crowd. Someone who understood the demands of motherhood and the pressure to lead her child in holiness. Someone who had been overcome with grief and sorrow. Someone whose purity did not make her immune to suffering, but rather intensified its pain.

In essence, I found all the answers to my desperate, burning questions. How can someone say yes to Jesus and live in a way that reflects him? What does it look like to be a holy woman? A holy wife? A holy mother? How can someone's life magnify Christ?

Mary.

She lived the answers.

Mary, then, not only proved to be relatable, but was *so* relatable that she was downright inspiring.

After all, I, too, have been falsely accused, grief-stricken, and lonely. I, too, have desperately desired to follow God and say yes to his will for my life. I, too, have longed to be a holy example to those around me.

And Mary did it all. Perfectly. But perfectly doesn't mean easily. No, the road Mary walked was a difficult one marked by many sorrows along the way, which only testifies to her spiritual toughness. She was tougher than I could ever dream to be. I mean, I grew up living and breathing elite athletics. I was trained from a young age to be physically and mentally tough. But spiritual toughness? I didn't even know what that meant. So, one night, Mary taught me herself.

There I was, soaking up the still silence in our home at the end of the night. My husband was working late, and after I'd put the kids down for bed, all I wanted was to plop down on the couch and watch a show or movie. One I could choose. One that starred real people instead of cartoons. A new one, I decided, about Mary. But as I got everything ready for rest and relaxation—including my own heart—I thought of the hamper of clean, unfolded clothes in my bedroom. I had done load after load of laundry throughout the day and had folded them all, save that last one. I knew what Mary—a mother inclined to perfect humility and charity—would do. She would make the sacrifice to serve her family, and she would do it with joy. The hamper, a constant thorn in my side, continued to beckon me.

"But, Mary," I whined, "the movie I was going to watch is about *you*. Isn't that good enough?"

"We must not simply watch it." Her words were as jolting as a right hook, yet as gentle as a caress. "We must live it."

In that moment, I understood. We cannot absorb virtue as passive witnesses. To be Christ-like, we must

Do what needs to be done.

work with God to build virtues within ourselves by putting them into action.

After all, could the greats—people like Leonardo da Vinci, William Shakespeare, Marie Curie, Michael Jordan, and Serena Williams—have risen to historical ranks in their fields if they had not dredged through countless hours of practice? Of course not. God gave them their passions and abilities, and they had to put their crafts to use in order to grow, develop, and perfect them.

The same is true with virtue. We don't merely absorb it through osmosis or gain it by passively observing others. No, developing virtue is a beautiful blend of God's grace merged with human effort. After all, God doesn't want to sit back and watch us go it alone. In fact, he knows we'd fail miserably if we tried to live virtuously all on our own. So instead, he helps us along this narrow path, generously pouring out his grace upon us through Baptism, and then giving us the spiritual gifts we need to continue the journey.

But we can't sit back and let God do all the work. Like a little child on a long journey, we must slip our hand into our Father's and walk with him. There may be times we feel exhausted or parched or lost. In those moments, we can cry out to God for what we need. Then, sustained by his grace, we can courageously set forth once again, putting God's gifts into action—pulling, tugging, yanking them forth from our spirit even when it's hard. Even when it's tiring. Even when it's the last thing we want to do and everything in us just wants to give up.

And, if we look closely enough, Mary shows us how to do that very thing.

In this book, we'll dive into Scripture and the life of one not-quite-so-saintly Catholic woman (ahem, me) to pull out the richness that makes Mary the greatest heroine to ever live.

Together, we'll examine the way Mary lived out the virtues as a God-loving woman, wife, and mother. Sounds a bit intimidating, but really, it's pretty simple. We'll walk through all of that together, one step at a time. Here's what you'll find in every chapter:

- ✦ *Scripture Verses*: take a glance at God's word and hear what he says about his own Blessed Mother

- ✦ *Real Life Stories*: read stories from my crazy life that have taught me more about Mary

- ✦ *A Soul That Magnifies*: take a closer look at how Mary lived out the virtues and learn how she can help us to do the same

- ✦ *Ponder in Your Heart*: ponder God's word with reflection/discussion questions

- ✦ *Fiat*: practice virtues through challenges so you can magnify the Lord, too

- ✦ *Prayer*: bring it all back to God through prayer.

I will continue to pray for you as we take Mary's hand and trek toward Jesus together. And, as our souls grow in virtue, I hope and pray that you, like Mary, will truly magnify the Lord.

SUBMISSION TO GOD'S WILL

The Annunciation

The angel said to her, "Do not be afraid, Mary, for you have found favor with God. And now, you will conceive in your womb and bear a son, and you will name him Jesus. He will be great, and will be called the Son of the Most High, and the Lord God will give to him the throne of his ancestor David. He will reign over the house of Jacob forever, and of his kingdom there will be no end." Mary said to the angel, "How can this be, since I am a virgin?" The angel said to her, "The Holy Spirit will come upon you, and the power of the Most High will overshadow you; therefore the child to be born will be holy, he will be called Son of God." Then Mary said, "Here am I, the servant of the Lord; let it be with me according to your word." Then the angel departed from her.

—LUKE 1:30–35, 38

PREGNANT.

The word was written, clear as day, at the end of the stick I held in my hand.

My knees buckled beneath me. I sank to the floor of our tiny bathroom. *Why? Why is this happening now?*

Inside my chest, my heart skipped and sprinted and hiccupped and faceplanted. I uncurled trembling fingers from the pink-and-white tool in my hand. The one covered in bodily waste.

Maybe I had misread it. Maybe it was a false positive. Maybe I could still have all the things I wanted.

I peeked back down.

Still pregnant.

My heart plummeted.

How would I ever rise from this spot in our broken-down shack that we could already barely afford? How would I be able to tell my husband that the financial stress we'd been under was about to get worse?

You gave us a BABY? I hissed angrily at God. *But I'm too young! And we haven't been married long enough. And I don't know the first thing about babies. And I was JUST starting my career. And we are broke.*

I rattled off a litany of reasons I couldn't do what he was asking me to do. Or rather, all the reasons I didn't *want* to do what he was asking me to do.

And yet, the answer remained the same.

I was officially a mother.

It got me thinking about another woman whose motherhood took her by surprise. Except this girl was a betrothed teenager living in a society that killed women for infidelity.

Still, she received the same word I did:

Mother.

The message was spoken, clear as day, by a glorious angel in the middle of a mundane day.

I wonder if Mary trembled, her knees buckling beneath her, as Gabriel spilled the beans. Inside her chest, Mary's heart may have skipped and sprinted and hiccupped and faceplanted.

How can this be since I've never, you know, done . . . the thing . . . that makes babies? the innocent Mary may have wondered to herself.

Maybe she had misheard. Maybe Gabriel had the wrong girl.

She dared a glance at his angelic face, and then asked her question out loud.

And, incredibly, the answer remained the same.

She would officially be a mother, if only she chose to accept it.

In that moment, all of heaven held its breath, awaiting Mary's consent to bring Salvation itself into the world.

There was so much to question. So much to ponder, to sort out. How easily she could have rattled off a litany of reasons she couldn't do what God was asking her to do. *But I'm too young! And Joseph! How will I be able to tell him that I'm pregnant? He'll leave me! And when others find out, they'll stone me to death!*

No one would've faulted her for it.

But, instead of falling to the floor, it seems like Mary steeled herself. She didn't need to question. For her, there was nothing to sort out. God chose her. God wanted her for this singular role in salvation history.

What more did she need to know?

Submission to God gave her strength.

After all, how could the almighty God who led an entire people out of slavery allow her one little life to slip through his fingers? How could the God who parted the waters—not once, but *several times*—be incapable of forging a way for her to press forward? How could the God who protected David when he was face-to-face with giants fail to protect her while she was cradling a tiny baby?

Perhaps in her great humility, she bowed her head before the angel Gabriel, ready to give her answer. Her yes. The competency of God outweighed any worldly doubt, and total trust—total submission to God's will—formed the famous words gathering on her tongue.

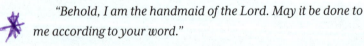

"Behold, I am the handmaid of the Lord. May it be done to me according to your word."

⚜ A Soul That Magnifies ⚜

Submission to God's Will

Nobody likes to hear the word "submit." It, like the word "surrender," has been falsely construed to signify weakness. But, when you think about it, we all submit to something, be it our governmental structure and law, our boss, our parents or spouse, or—most easily—our own desires. Sometimes we submit to more than one thing at a time. Everything we do is based in submission to *something*.

Mary, however, was constantly submitting herself to God, and God alone.

And submission to God is not for the faint of heart. It is not a passive activity nor is it a sign of frailty. Rather, submission to God takes strength and self-discipline, wisdom and courage. It takes immense amounts of power and self-control to set down your own wants and plans when God calls you to something else. To cast off doubt and worry. To trust that God knows what he's doing (and even that he knows better than us!).

No, submission does not mean weakness. Submission—especially submission to God's will—requires everything inside us, as well as the courage to give everything we have in service to God instead of self.

When the angel Gabriel presented Mary with her singular role in salvation history, it was really God asking, "Will you trust me even if people mock you? Even if your husband spurns and divorces you? Even if it costs you your life, stone by agonizing stone?"

Mary's answer—without hesitation—was yes.

Because Mary knows that the only gift we truly possess—the only thing we own completely and can give to God—is the gift of our own free will. And, every time the opportunity arose, she willingly chose to give it to him.

Ponder in Your Heart

1. Reread the story of the Annunciation (Luke 1:26–38). How did Mary surrender to God's will? What do you imagine was going through her head in that moment?

2. What is God asking you to trust him with today?

3. How can you give God your own fiat—your own "yes"—to that call? How can you be a "handmaid of the Lord" right now, in this moment?

4. Reread Luke 1:38, but this time as you read it, declare it as a personal promise to God.

Prayer

Mary, thank you for being a constant example of what it looks like to say yes to God. Before Jesus had even manifested himself in human form, you accepted him. You said yes to him, and in doing so, you became the world's first Christian. Pray for us now, Holy Mother, that we, too, may have the strength to lay down any wants and desires that are apart from his. Pray that we may always choose the better portion—your Divine Son—and trust that his ways are better than our own. Be by our side when we're tempted to submit to something other than God, and lead us in the way of eternal salvation. Amen.

CHARITY

The Visitation

> In those days Mary set out and went with haste to a
> Judean town in the hill country, where she entered
> the house of Zechariah and greeted Elizabeth.
>
> —LUKE 1:39–40

Stunning. The silence was stunning. The past fifteen
hours had been full of noise, toddler tantrums, and
fights.

So when my kids finally went to sleep, I gulped down
the silence like a madman lapping up water in the
desert.

Soaking it in, I raced toward the bookshelf and tilted
one of the books into my hand. It was a book I'd been
reading for weeks. My bookmark peeked out from
somewhere near the end. My heart danced, a smile
spreading across my face as I remembered the excitement of the story. The beautiful writing. I was *so close* to

the grand finale! Soon, I'd know how the main character got out of his seemingly escape-less situation.
Anticipation hummed in my fingertips, and my heart
sang as I flopped onto the couch.

As I devoured the words, my husband plopped
down beside me, his computer perched on his lap. He
was preparing for a big presentation he had at work the
next day. One he'd been piecing and splicing together
for quite a while, trying to make it perfect.

He turned to look at me. "Would you mind listening
to my speech?" he asked.

"Sure." My heart ached as I placed the bookmark
back, pausing the story mid-chapter.

My husband gave his speech. I laughed. He cracked
his jokes. I laughed harder. Then the dryer buzzed and I
cried a little inside.

The shirt my husband was going to wear for his presentation was in that load. And, of course, it needed to
be ironed, but my husband was already knee-deep in
his own project. One he had clearly been working very
hard on.

I just wanted to read, for heaven's sake. To have time
to myself after fifteen hours of the opposite. The desire
was so deep—so palpable—it threatened to suffocate me.
After all, self-care is just as important as serving others.
It would totally be okay to take the break I craved and
regain my wits a bit. Paralyzed, I tried to figure out

which course of action I should take in this moment. Self-care or service to another?

The itch to open my book and keep reading nagged at my fingers. I clenched my teeth.

"Will reading that book change your life?" I could almost feel Mary shrug beside me. "Probably not. Will setting aside your own desires to help someone else change your life? Yes." She gave me the answers in an instant, revealing how one single act of charity—however small—would not only alleviate the weight of my husband's cross, but also contribute to the perfection of my own soul.

And *that* really would be life changing.

Kind of like how she went out of her way to take care of her cousin. How, in the first trimester of pregnancy, she poured herself out in service to someone else. And she didn't just *go*. She went *with haste*. She didn't spend time obsessing over what she wanted but instead focused on setting aside her own desires to serve someone in need. She literally traveled across the country to alleviate the weight of her cousin's cross.

All I had to do was rub out a few wrinkles.

So why did it seem like the laundry room was so far away?

Of course, I could have read my book and let my husband fend for himself. And, knowing my husband, he wouldn't have thought anything of it. He would have stayed up as late as it took to do what needed to be done.

But. I could also choose to bring heaven to earth. I could *choose* to make God's Kingdom come.

Read or iron. Do what feels good or what feels sacrificial. Me or my husband.

The choice was mine. It was simple, but not easy.

I flicked one more glance at my husband. His lips silently mouthed the words he'd spent weeks writing. His brow pinched in anxiety.

Then, thanks to Mary, I set my book down and joyfully went to get the iron.

❧ A Soul That Magnifies ❧

Charity

Mary did something radical. She served BIG. It probably took several days of dusty, dirty, dangerous travel to get to the hill country of Judea, and she did it while in the first trimester of pregnancy just so she could put herself in the service of someone else.

We can serve in big ways like that, too, if God so calls us, but we can also bring charity—love in action—into the little moments. The mundane moments. The every day. The *right now*.

Mary served in those seemingly unseen, mostly mundane ways as well. As baby Jesus grew inside her during those three months, Mary continued to take care of Elizabeth and Zechariah. She probably cooked, cleaned, mopped the floors, and maybe even rubbed the wrinkles out of their clothes. Because even small acts, when done with great love, are big in God's eyes.

Even now, I remember so much about that night beside my husband. The way the stress melted from his face, a smile breaking through the nerves, as I walked into the living room with the ironing board and his button-down shirt. I remember the tilt of his head, the way the corners of his lips turned down, truly touched that I would serve him. The genuine joy in his voice when he thanked me.

And the book I was reading? I've racked my brains, and I can't for the life of me even remember the title, let alone the grand finale.

Your actions don't have to change the whole world. Charity can be as small as a smile or a kind word. It could be sacrificing a want to fulfill someone else's need. Heck, it could be as simple as asking someone how they're doing and then truly caring about the answer.

Anything, really. Charity could be anything, as long as you are looking and loving, seeing and serving those around you.

For even one single act of charity—no matter the size—will alleviate the weight of your neighbor's cross and also contribute to the perfection of your own soul.

Ponder in Your Heart

1. What aspect(s) of charity do you excel at? What do you find to be a struggle?

2. We can only love as much as we're willing to inconvenience ourselves for another. Can you think of a time when you chose to set your own wants aside to serve the needs of someone else? How can you be more open to letting yourself be inconvenienced in order to serve others?

3. Reread Luke 1:39–40, 56. How much does Mary inconvenience herself to take care of Elizabeth? What does that say about the amount of love she had for her cousin?

Fiat

Be on the lookout for ways you can put God's love into action, and then do something to joyfully serve someone else.

Prayer

Mary, thank you for always being here for us, loving us, serving us, and leading us ever closer to Heaven. You never tire of doing good. Even when you walked this earth, you placed others before yourself and put God above all. Pray that we may model the ardent charity you so beautifully displayed thousands of years ago and still give to this day. Please ask your Son to fill us with the strength to deny ourselves and choose love, even when it's hard. Lord Jesus, give me a heart willing to inconvenience myself for others. Amen.

PIETY

Blessed Are You

When Elizabeth heard Mary's greeting, the child leaped in her womb. And Elizabeth was filled with the Holy Spirit and exclaimed with a loud cry, "Blessed are you among women, and blessed is the fruit of your womb. And why has this happened to me, that the mother of my Lord comes to me? For as soon as I heard the sound of your greeting, the child in my womb leaped for joy."

—Luke 1:41–44

Not long after my wedding, I grabbed some coffee and a bite to eat with my bridesmaids. Together, we gathered around a small table in the café and the conversation steered back to that magical night. I couldn't stop smiling as we recounted every single detail.

The way the air itself seemed to pulse with raw energy and unbridled joy.

The way a little girl I had never met from my husband's side of the family slipped her hand in mine and asked if she could dance with the princess.

The way my maid of honor stuffed herself into a tiny bathroom stall with me, lifting up enormous volumes of material on my dress so I could use the toilet.

The way my uncle danced—one hand on his belly, the other hand wagging one finger in the air—to every single song. For hours.

The way one of the guests had sat back, taking everything in. "I've been to a lot of weddings, but this one is different," he said. "Why is that?"

Well, because the Holy Spirit was *on fire* that night, that's why.

Everything about that night was perfect.

"You know," one of the ladies piped up and took a quick swig of coffee. "I really liked the best man's speech. It was cool how he said his favorite quality about your husband is his faith."

I nodded along, puffed with pride in my new hubby. The way he lived out his faith was something that attracted me to him as well. It was beautiful. Just being around my husband made me fall more deeply in love with God.

I smiled inside. *That's my man.*

Another bridesmaid nodded at me. "I never knew faith was that important to you."

Oof.

She didn't know faith was important to me? This, my *bridesmaid*, a woman I handpicked to walk beside me as I prepared for the sacrament of Holy Matrimony?

I tried not to double over in the coffee shop as I wrestled with that in my heart. I trusted these women to help me on the toilet, but I didn't let them into my faith life? Something about that was wrong.

How could they not know I loved God?

The answer was quite clear. I didn't show it. I didn't live it out. Heck, I didn't really know *how* to live it out. Most of the people I surrounded myself with didn't know God, and I hated confrontation as much as I loved Jesus.

So I kept my love for him under wraps. Faith, to me, was a private endeavor. I loved Jesus, sure, but I didn't want to rock anyone's boat, so I kept him all to myself and never spoke of him to anyone.

Mary, on the other hand? Her piety—her reverence and devotion to God—was evident.

Mary's heart was so steeped in God—so full of Love— that when the angel Gabriel told her she would be the Mother of God and that her cousin, Elizabeth, was also pregnant, Mary somehow focused on the part about Elizabeth.

And, somehow, after days of dirty and possibly dangerous travel, Mary was still so completely full of piety, her "hello" was saturated with the Holy Spirit.

Unlike mine, Mary's faith and love for God were on full display in every word and every deed.

Piety was such a palpable, tangible part of who she was, it transformed her and the people around her. God was so present within Mary, a single word from her was enough to open the people around her to be filled with the Holy Spirit.

I sit now with my Bible, taking everything in, noticing how Mary is not quite like anyone else. *I've met a lot of people, but this one is different*, I think as I read about her. *Why is that?*

Well, because the Holy Spirit is on fire with her, that's why.

⚜ A Soul That Magnifies ⚜

Piety

Mary's life was so completely entwined with God, it may have been hard to see where her story ended and his began at times. From the very beginning, I imagine her parents may have noticed something different about their little girl. Something special. Something holy. Surely her piety set her apart, even at a young age. After all, in a fallen world—even among God's own chosen people—it would be hard to *not* notice someone who is full of grace. Maybe she even found it difficult to make friends because she was so different. Yet, she remained virtuous even when she didn't fit in. Then, as she grew and matured, her piety never wavered. Never dipped or rebelled during her pre-pubescent or teenage years. If anything, it shone even brighter.

After all, there she was, a teenager housing the great I AM inside her very own body. She then, the living tabernacle, probably couldn't help but radiate God's joy and love. Holiness saturated her demeanor and disposition so much, Elizabeth noticed her piety before Mary said more than one word.

We too can live piously, but we have to be willing to be different. To not fit in. After all, piety has the tendency to set us apart from the world.

Like Mary, we don't even have to speak to shine with piety. Our reverence and devotion to God can seep into the world through the way we live.

A willingness to serve. A loving greeting, genuinely caring about how someone else is doing. A passionate, uninhibited pursuit of Jesus. A love for him so deep and rich, you *want* to bring him to others.

For after receiving Jesus in Communion, we, too, become living tabernacles. As we house the great I AM inside our very own bodies, we can radiate his joy and love. And, hopefully, our lives can become so completely entwined with God, it will be hard to see where his story ends and ours begins.

Ponder in Your Heart

1. How can you live in a way that makes your faith stand out? How would you explain to others what makes you set apart?

2. How are the people in your life affected by you? How are you affected by them? Do you bring each other closer to or farther from Jesus?

3. Reread Luke 1:41–44. What does piety look like? How can it become transformative in your life?

Fiat

Let other people know you love Jesus, simply by how you live.

Prayer

Mary, your spirit was so immersed in God that simply being around you drew other people closer to him. Pray for me, Mother, that God may be so present in my soul that he can touch others through my voice. Pray for me, that my soul may be so steeped in God, it transforms me into a new creation—one full of love, hope, and joy. Pray for me to have the courage to stand out for him, especially in a world that so desperately needs to know him. Lord Jesus, your love is magnetic and beautiful. Please give me the grace of piety, so that I may live and love in a way that transforms and draws people closer to you. Amen.

HUMILITY

The Magnificat

And Mary said, "My soul magnifies the Lord, and my spirit rejoices in God my Savior, for he has looked with favor on the lowliness of his servant. Surely, from now on all generations will call me blessed; for the Mighty One has done great things for me, and holy is his name. His mercy is for those who fear him from generation to generation. He has shown strength with his arm; he has scattered the proud in the thoughts of their hearts. He has brought down the powerful from their thrones, and lifted up the lowly; he has filled the hungry with good things, and sent the rich away empty. He has helped his servant Israel, in remembrance of his mercy, according to the promise he made to our ancestors, to Abraham and to his descendants forever."

—LUKE 1:46–55

I was born with basketball in my blood.

Legend has it that, when I was two years old, I got my first "orange ball," and by the time I was three, I was dribbling laps around regulation-sized courts.

Ugh. Just saying that out loud makes me cringe.

You see, it breaks a cardinal rule from my upbringing.

Be humble. That's what I'd always been taught. *Don't get a big head.* And to be humble, I thought, you've got to reject compliments. Say you're no good. Do whatever it takes to show that, no, you don't have that strength or skill. No one actually *said* that, of course, but that's how I internalized it.

By the time I was in my first year of high school, I had spent fourteen years living and breathing basketball. I shot hoops every day after school and ran myself through ballhandling drills just for fun. With that God-given passion combined with my psycho-like obsession with the sport, I became a pretty good basketball player.

Not that I'd ever admit that out loud, of course. I had also spent fourteen years rejecting compliments.

When tryouts for the high school's varsity basketball team came, the week went by in a giddy blur. The floor vibrated below our feet as dozens of balls crashed to the floor and bounced back to our fingertips. The air heaved with heavy breaths, whistles, and shouts of direction.

It was my happy place.

Then came the day of reckoning, when cuts were made and the teams finalized. I sat cross-legged at half-court surrounded by hundreds of anxious girls as we all awaited our fate.

One of my closest friends scooted close, her bright red ponytail swishing as she nudged my shoulder. "You're going to make varsity," she whispered, smiling.

I know. I've been training with them for months now. That's what I thought to myself, at least. I would never say such an arrogant thing out loud. So instead, I shook my head at my friend. "No, I'm not."

"Yes, you are," she pressed, practically singing the words. "Just wait. They're going to call your name and you're going to be a *freshman* on *varsity*."

"Nah." I feigned a blush and turned my attention to the coaches as they taped The List on the wall. Out of the hundreds of girls in this gym, only a dozen or so would make the cut.

"If your name is on this list," the coach shouted in her typical booming voice, "then welcome to the team." Then she walked away, leaving The List all alone on the wall.

My friend grabbed my arm and pulled me to my feet, hustling me over. Together, we scoured the names.

Right there, smack dab in the middle of the list, was my name.

A freshman on varsity.

"Look!" she pointed to my name with joy, despite the fact that hers was nowhere to be found. "I *told* you you'd make it!"

Even then, my first reaction was to deny it. *Ah, I probably won't play much. Maybe it was a mistake. A fluke.*

But I was too tired and too thrilled to speak. So I simply stared at my name, smiling, allowing my friend to wrap her arms around my neck.

True humility, I know now, has nothing to do with rejecting compliments. When we reject a compliment, we disown and ignore a God-given gift. If we view compliments as acknowledging God's gifts within us, it's actually humble to *accept* those affirmations. When we accept them in that way, we can recognize God's goodness and thank him for giving us that gift.

Mary understood that.

So when an angel appeared to Mary and addressed her with reverence, she was troubled, but didn't deny it. She didn't feign a blush. Instead, she took it as an opportunity to learn more about God and the marvelous things he was up to.

And when Elizabeth gushed about how "blessed" Mary is, the young girl didn't refute the title. (A title *much* more impressive than being a freshman on varsity!)

Because of Mary's true humility, Elizabeth never had to come back and say, "I *told* you that you were blessed among women! I *told* you that you were the mother of my Lord!"

By accepting the compliment and turning the praise to God, Mary shifted the focus off of herself and away from Elizabeth, to the One who truly deserves the attention and adoration. Through their true humility, the two women could move forward, growing more in love with God and his goodness.

❦ A Soul That Magnifies ❦

Humility

True humility isn't disowning or denying our God-given gifts. It's recognizing and even celebrating those gifts with the understanding that they are, in fact, gifts. Gifts that have been given by an all-powerful and all-loving Father.

Humility, then, is understanding, accepting, and appreciating that God stitched together every single detail that makes us, *us*. He's done everything. If we have a talent or strength, it's because he gave it to us. The rightful praise, then, should go to him for giving us everything we have.

When I learned to accept compliments and use them to praise God, affirmations finally satisfied my heart. I started to hope people would recognize my gifts, not so *I* could be praised, but so that I could turn that into worship of God.

What I learned in my thirties about humility, Mary had a firm grasp on by early adolescence. Because she was truly humble, the lady couldn't receive a compliment without launching into a full song of praise to God. Because God made her. He had done everything for her. She knew that. And even today, any praise we give to Mary, she rightfully turns into praise for the One who created her.

Ponder in Your Heart

1. God created you intricately, purposefully, and uniquely (see Psalm 139). Spend some time identifying the gifts that God gave you. What are some of those gifts that make you, *you*?

2. How can you use those gifts in a way that's pleasing to God?

3. Reread Luke 1:26–38 or Luke 1:39–56. In the first reading, Gabriel meets Mary with a reverent greeting and then calls her "favored one." In the second, Elizabeth exclaims loudly and repeatedly calls Mary "blessed." How does Mary recognize and celebrate her God-given gifts and turn that into praise of God? How can you do that, too?

Fiat

Accept a compliment and turn it into praise of God.

Prayer

My spirit rejoices in you, my God, and my soul wishes to proclaim your greatness. But sometimes I get caught up in pursu-

ing my own greatness. When I am tempted to fuel my own ego, remind me of my littleness. When I marvel at the wonders of this world, inspire me to dream bigger. To set my sights higher. To keep my eyes upon you, upon Heaven. Help me understand who I am in relation to you, God, and help me see you in all my skills, passions, and strengths, for they are all gifts from you. All praise rightfully belongs to you. Inspire me, Lord, to work together with you, taking the gifts you've given me and working hard to grow them, refine them, and give them to others in service and love. Mary, pray for me, that I may sing of God's goodness as easily and effortlessly as you do. Amen.

FORTITUDE

Traveling to Bethlehem

Joseph also went from the town of Nazareth in Galilee to Judea, to the city of David called Bethlehem,
because he was descended from the house and family of David. He went to be registered with Mary,
to whom he was engaged and who was expecting a
child. While they were there, the time came for her to
deliver her child. And she gave birth to her firstborn
son and wrapped him in bands of cloth, and laid him
in a manger, because there was no place for them in
the inn.

—Luke 2:4–7

Where I live, it takes forty-five minutes to get everywhere.

When we first moved here, I joked with my husband
about the lengthy distances and the fact that I needed
the GPS to get to the grocery store.

My husband was used to it, of course, since this is his hometown, and all the time in the car was fine with me—I actually kind of liked the driving.

There was only one problem.

I was six months pregnant with our second child. And guess how far away the hospital was?

Forty-five minutes.

As the clock ticked down to my impending due date, that forty-five-minute drive started to feel more like a vast ocean. Day after day, I panicked about the reality that I might not make it to the hospital in time. And, every day for weeks, small contractions threw my world into a tailspin.

Is this it? I'd stop everything I was doing to evaluate my contraction. *Is this the real deal? Is my water going to break? Oh good Lord, I bet my water is going to break. Should I get in the car right now and book it?!*

Surely, I made everyone around me nervous, as they watched this hugely pregnant woman freeze like a statue with a horrified look on her face. But, time and again, the contraction would fade, and I'd be left, keys in hand, painless. Contractionless. Laborless.

Then my worst nightmares came true. Labor began when I was at home with my one-year-old while my husband was at work. Forty-five minutes away.

This time the labor pains didn't go away. They intensified.

I called my husband. No answer.

I called my in-laws. No answer.

I called my sister-in-law. No answer.

In a panicked rush, I scooped up my one-year-old and stuffed her into her car seat. "It's you and me, kiddo," I said, latching her buckle and wincing through another contraction. "You might end up having to catch this baby. You're okay with that, right?"

She looked up at me, her wide smile in no way reflecting the terror I felt inside.

I hopped into the driver's seat, white-knuckling the steering wheel, and, together with my toddler, started the trek to the hospital.

What if there's an accident on one of the highways, like there so often is? What if there's traffic? What if I can't get ahold of anyone?

What if? What if? What if?

Of course, God took care of everything. My mother-in-law met me halfway and drove the rest of the way to the hospital. My sister-in-law met us at the hospital and helped me check in. Then my husband raced in to hold my hand and rub my back until the baby was born.

All my worrying had been in vain.

And then there was Mary.

Mary, who, when asked to travel to another *city*, for goodness's sake, got her hugely pregnant self on a donkey and went.

It took four *days* to get from Nazareth to Bethlehem. By donkey. Over hills. And there was no hospital at the end of her journey. No zooming cars, long highways. No cushiony seats or air conditioning or heat. No shelter from rain or winter weather.

And yet, she was asked to do something, so she rolled up her sleeves and got to work. Because, man, that lady was tough. Tough in spirit, to be sure. Nothing could shake her unwavering faith and trust in God, and because of that, Mary could (and did) endure whatever life threw at her.

She traveled for four days—by DONKEY—while at some point going into labor.

She humbly adapted in the unfamiliar town, giving birth in the filth of animals.

Then she fled for her life—and the life of her child—when an immature, blood-thirsty ruler hunted her baby.

She lived as a refugee in a foreign country, with only her husband and newborn by her side, all while trying to figure out this whole new mom thing.

She understood the pressure of little eyes watching her every move (and her kid was *God*, for heaven's sake!).

And that was before the *really* difficult stuff happened.

Stuff like the initiation of her Son's controversial ministry.

Stuff like her Son trekking into the desert—alone—to go toe-to-toe with Satan.

Stuff like watching her Son get whipped to bloody shreds, and then nailed to a tree, naked, abandoned, and dejected.

And she remained close to God through it all, her fortitude radiating each time she chose to trust him.

Heck, *I* can't even remain holy when one of my kids wets their bed.

Because let's face it, being a holy woman is hard. And Mary did it better than anyone else.

She's not the weak, passive figure I once imagined. No, Mary was by and large one of the toughest people this world has ever seen. Hers was a real fortitude, the kind rooted deep in her soul instead of on the knuckles of her fist. Because she was firmly anchored in God, she could bravely face whatever the world threw her way.

❦ A Soul That Magnifies ❦

Fortitude

My favorite types of movies are those with tough heroines—the ones who can take a punch and keep fighting. The ones who are strong and fierce. The ones who inspire me to go out into the world and kick butt for justice, too.

Though it's cool to watch these women kick some tail, especially in the pursuit of goodness, that's not the toughness we should aspire to. It's not necessarily toughness at all. After all, it's actually easy to throw a punch when you're mad. (In a surge of fury, I once spiked a water bottle into the ground, bending its lip and rendering it useless. Ironically, that surge of "toughness" left me feeling embarrassed and ashamed, not empowered like the women on screen seem to be.)

Fortitude—true spiritual toughness—involves not only the courage to face external danger or difficulty, but also the ability to conquer oneself (see Prov 16:32). It's *way* harder to show self-restraint when angry, trust when anxious, gratitude when you have little, and humility when you're tempted to put yourself first. That kind of toughness can only come through a strong, virtuous spirit strengthened by God's grace, and boy, Mary had *heaps* of that. And that kind of toughness? It actually *does* leave you feeling refreshed, renewed, and empowered.

So Mary was a billion times tougher than these fictional movie characters. Her strength didn't stem from a sleek body, toned with taut muscle. No, her fortitude was rooted more deeply than flesh and bone. It resided at her very core. In her spirit. A spirit so totally consumed by her love of God—and God's love for her—that it produced true, ascetic strength. *That's* the kind of tenacity we, as Christians, should pursue.

Ponder in Your Heart

1. *When the going gets tough, the tough get going*, or so they say. How can you "get going" and show fortitude in your own life today?

2. Athletes train their bodies through exercise and a healthy diet to become physically strong. How can you train your soul to get stronger? What training plan can you and God come up with together?

3. Reread Luke 2:4–7 and imagine all the hardships Mary and Joseph had to endure. How did they demonstrate fortitude during the tough times?

Fiat

Which sinful habits do you struggle with the most? Pick one—just one—even if it's small. Now, your mission—should you choose to accept it—is to work with God to destroy that sin in your life. Make a concerted effort to form an opposite good habit to combat that sin.

It will not be easy. It will require fortitude. You must be humble enough to acknowledge what you lack and ask God to provide it, and also courageous enough to put his gifts into practice. So, gird your loins and steel your heart for battle. Arm yourself with your Bible, the rosary, and frequent trips to Mass and Reconciliation. Ask Mary to cover you with her intercession. Maybe even journal through this process. Whatever you do, stay close to God and pray, pray, pray, so that, together with him, you can roundhouse kick that sin in the face.

With God's help, we can take steps to overcome sins, but it's an ongoing fight. Some days, we may see victory. Other days, we may lose the battle. But take heart and remember that Jesus has already won the war.

Prayer

Mary, I want to be spiritually tough like you. Please pray for me that Jesus, the One who has overcome the whole world, will be my comrade in arms and conquer the sin in my life. Where there is selfishness, may he sow humility. Where there is fear, trust. When my heart is hurt or angry, pray that he may subdue me with self-restraint and forgiveness. Through his grace, may I increase in fortitude—the toughness of a strong spirit rooted deeply in God—so that I may be liberated from my sinful chains and choose, instead, the freedom that comes from him. And when I fail, pray that I may have the strength to get back up and try again. Amen.

ADORATION OF JESUS

The Nativity

When the angels had left them and gone into heaven, the shepherds said to one another, "Let us go now to Bethlehem and see this thing that has taken place, which the Lord has made known to us." So they went with haste and found Mary and Joseph, and the child lying in the manger. When they saw this, they made known what had been told them about this child; and all who heard it were amazed at what the shepherds told them.

—Luke 2:15–18

When [the wise men] saw that the star had stopped, they were overwhelmed with joy. On entering the house, they saw the child with Mary his mother; and they knelt down and paid him homage. Then, opening their treasure chests, they offered him gifts of gold, frankincense, and myrrh.

—Matthew 2:10–11

I've spent the last two weeks staring at my newborn.

I don't mean to. It just happens.

I coo at her as she nurses, in awe of the way her body draws life from mine. She snuggles in close after feeding, and I can't help but admire the sweet curve of her nose, the way her lips slide sideways in a smile, her tiny fingers that wrap themselves around mine.

Everything. I adore it all.

There are times I sit there, doing nothing but watching her, and completely lose track of time. It's times like those when all I want is to wrap her in my arms and never let go.

And it's times like those when Mary totally knocks my socks off.

I bet after Jesus' birth, Mary lovingly gazed upon him the way I look at my newborn. Perhaps she spent the first two weeks of his life simply staring at him. She might not have intended for it to happen that way. It just did. Perhaps while he drank the milk from her body, she whispered stories of how he delivered her people to the land of milk and honey. Maybe she wondered how someone so sleepy would awaken the whole world. Maybe she found it difficult to comprehend how such a tiny body could host the great I AM. And when he snuggled in close to her after feeding, I bet Mary couldn't help but admire the way his lips slid sideways in a smile and his tiny fingers wrapped themselves around hers.

Everything. She adored it all.

Perhaps it was times like those when all she wanted was to wrap him in her arms and never let go.

But she did. She did let go.

She endured scorn, ridicule, judgment, and even danger of death because of her pregnancy. Then, she encountered the hardships of traveling and perhaps yet another giant slap-in-the-face spurn from those of her husband's hometown as they, one after the other, refused to give her shelter. All to bring this baby into the world. And when the baby was finally here—when she *finally* found the One she belonged with, the One who would never scorn, deride, or abandon her—what was the first thing she did?

She shared him with others so they could worship and adore him.

When the shepherds rushed in—no doubt smelling of sweat and animals and outside air—and told her all about how they saw angels in the sky who directed them to this very manger? She held Jesus out for them to see and worship.

And when the wise men came, draped in the finest jewels and attire from the East—a culture vastly different from that of God's chosen people—and showered the baby with expensive gifts? She could have kept the Messiah to herself and her people, but instead, she lifted Baby Jesus up to let the Gentiles adore him.

Against every fiber in her motherly heart that may have screamed to hold Jesus close, she held him out for all to see.

After all, Jesus did not come solely for her, but for everyone—be it low or high ranking, Jew or gentile. He came for *everyone*.

So Mary held him out. She shared Jesus with the shepherds. With the magi. With *us*.

Because that is who she is. It is her legacy. She's the tabernacle made of flesh. A living, breathing monstrance. The constant finger that points the world to her Son.

❧ A Soul That Magnifies ❧

Adoration of Jesus

Adore.

When I hear that word, I think of fawning over something cute. To *ooh* and *ahh* over something adorable. Like little babies. So, it makes sense that Mary, Joseph, the shepherds, and the Magi would adore baby Jesus. Surely, he was adorable.

But what about when Jesus grew up? It's kind of strange to think about adoring a grown man. But that's exactly what Mary did. That lady never stopped adoring Jesus.

She adored him at the moment of his conception. She adored him when he was born. She adored him as a toddler and a teen. And yes, she even adored him as an adult. And we can, too.

Adoring something isn't merely melting at its cuteness. To adore someone *really* means to love, respect, and honor them in the highest possible degree. It means to admire or worship.

So now, we can adore Jesus through devout prayer. We can adore him by the way we dress and participate in Mass. We can adore him by approaching the tabernacle and the Eucharist with great care and reverence.

Heck, in the Catholic Church, we have time set apart specifically for gathering at Jesus' feet and adoring him. Fittingly, it's called Adoration.

Being adorable, then, doesn't just mean being cute. It means being worthy of love, respect, honor, and worship. By *that* definition, Jesus is the most adorable person who ever existed.

Ponder in Your Heart

1. Have you ever thought of Jesus as adorable? How can you adore Jesus today?

2. How can you hold him out and share him with others?

3. Reread Luke 2:15–18 and Matthew 2:10–11. How is Mary like the monstrance during Adoration?

Fiat

Schedule a time to go to Adoration and spend some time adoring Christ in the Blessed Sacrament. Thank Mary for holding him out to you—for holding him out *for* you—so that you can experience his splendor and love. Receive Jesus with wonder and awe as the shepherds and wise men did upon first seeing him. Let him fill your heart with complete and genuine love of him, and then, like Mary, go out into the world and share him with others.

Prayer

I adore you, Jesus, though sometimes my love for you falls flat. Sometimes I take you for granted. When that happens, remind me of your majesty—of your infinite goodness and love—and fill me once again with awe. Make me like the shepherds, who on that very first Christmas couldn't wait to get to the manger to catch a glimpse of you. Make me like the wise men, who would gladly go out of their way to find and adore you. Mother Mary, thank you for holding Jesus out to me, that I may worship and adore him. Lord, I kneel before you now and offer you the gift of my heart. Amen.

CONTEMPLATION

She Kept All These Things in Her Heart

All who heard it were amazed at what the shepherds told them. But Mary treasured all these words and pondered them in her heart.

—LUKE 2:18–19

It was Black Friday.

And, like every other Friday in the Gillespy household, it was Donut Friday.

My husband and I corralled the kids, loaded them into the car, and headed straight for our favorite donut shop.

And, as it turned out, our destiny.

A woman, no older than me, stood on the curb as my husband and I unloaded our tiny tots from their car seats. Her short, wavy brown hair bobbed above her shoulders as she waited there for someone.

For us, actually.

"Um . . . excuse me," she said as we walked toward the smell of melt-in-your-mouth sugar. "Do you believe in Jesus?"

Inside, I rolled my eyes. *Oh no*, I thought, *here's another person who's come to tell me about the end of times being near and how I should repent or spend eternity in a lake of fire.*

But, of course, that's not what I said.

I believe the words that actually came out of my mouth were saturated in some sort of unexpected southern drawl (which happens when I'm nervous) and sounded more like, "Yes ma'am, we sure do."

"My name's Courtney." She extended her hand and we exchanged introductions. "Did you know Jesus is coming back soon? Like, *really* soon?"

Yep, definitely one of those curbside brimstone and fire preachers. Let's cut this short before she gives me a pamphlet for her church.

Then she pointed a finger directly at me. "God sent me here—to this spot—and wanted me to tell you that he is going to use you in a big way."

Bumps leapt to the surface of my skin, and my hairs stood on end beside them. My insides felt alive somehow, tingling and buzzing with new energy. This was much different than what I expected. When was she going to start selling us on joining her church? Where was her propaganda pamphlet? When should I start shielding my children?

Emotion—something like joy mixed with admiration—misted in her cerulean eyes as she held my gaze. "You are a BIG part of his plan. You and your children."

That was it. That was the message. My destiny.

I grappled with those words, unsure what they meant, as I tried to process them there on the sidewalk. Thoughts forced themselves through my sludge-like brain.

Is this Courtney lady really a curbside preacher like I originally thought? Is she a prophet? Is she completely nuts?

What did she mean, God's going to use me in a big way? What does "big" mean to Jesus—the One who taught that the last will be first?

What did she mean that Jesus will come back soon? And what's "soon" to God, to whom one day is a thousand years and a thousand years is like a day?

Why was I dumbstruck, unable to speak, as my hair stood on end and my heart hummed with life inside me?

I wanted to ask those questions, but when I looked back, Courtney was gone.

I wonder if, like me, Mary ever stood in one spot, paralyzed by pondering.

According to Scripture, she contemplated just about everything.

Over and over again, that's what Mary did. She's quoted rarely, but seems to think deeply, wrestling with it all and turning it over in her heart. I can only imagine the inner workings of her mind, ever focused on finding God's meaning in each scrap of life.

What do these shepherds mean they "saw a choir of angels in the sky"?

What does it mean that the angels revealed this knowledge to shepherds, of all people?

What does it mean that the great I AM is resting in a manger?

What will the world look like now that our Messiah is here, in the flesh? What sorts of things will happen to give glory to God and peace to men?

I can only imagine all the things she contemplated as she raised Jesus. Heck, I constantly wonder what in the world my kids are thinking and doing, and they're not God.

She must've had a lot to sort through, but she never let the busyness or craziness of life strip her of each memory or the fact that each moment with Jesus had meaning. But what *was* that meaning? What was God trying to teach her? What was he trying to teach the world? She refused to let anything slip.

So she kept everything—*everything*—in her heart, hoping to watch God slip the pieces gloriously together to reveal the bigger picture of his plan.

❧ A Soul That Magnifies ❧

Contemplation

I have kept that encounter with Courtney in my heart, wrestling with it and turning it over and over, trying to match it up with God's daily call for my life. So far, I haven't been able to make heads or tails of it.

And that really drives me nuts.

After all, we live in an age when, if we don't know something, we simply Google it and *voilà*! In seconds, we have all our answers at our fingertips.

But to contemplate? Ugh. That takes work. It takes time. It requires patience. It allows the risk of being wrong, at least for a moment.

And boy, I don't like that. I want to know things, and I want to know them *now*. Not knowing something—and having to *wait* for the answer?—makes me feel all squirmy inside.

But I always keep that exchange in the back of my mind in case I finally encounter the other piece of my life's puzzle that clicks perfectly in its grooves. I believe it's out there somewhere, that moment that gives this message clarity and helps reveal God's bigger picture.

That's exactly what Mary did. She spent her entire life mulling things over. Puzzling. Piecing. Striving to better understand God and his plan. She sought the heart—God's heart—in everything. Her memories never got lost or discarded. And boy, it's a good thing Mary held on to those moments throughout her life, turning them over in her heart as she did—because, over time, Jesus handed her the pieces that helped paint a clearer picture of his very own Sacred Heart.

What did it mean that the angels revealed this knowledge to shepherds? Well, the last will be first and the first will be last (see Matthew 20:16), and God reveals things to the lowly while keeping them hidden from the learned (see Matthew 11:25).

What did it mean that the great I AM rested in a feeding place for animals? Well, Jesus is the Bread of Life and commanded that we eat of his body (see John 6:51).

What would the world look like now that our Messiah was here, in the flesh? What sorts of things would happen to give glory to God and peace to men? By golly, Mary spent her whole life witnessing those answers play out.

Now, thanks to Jesus coming to pave the way, we also get to live and participate in God's salvific plan. And when we are handed a puzzle piece of that plan for our lives, we can treasure it in our hearts until we find another that matches its grooves.

Ponder in Your Heart

1. What is the difference between thinking and contemplating? Why would contemplating be virtuous?

2. When was the last time you pondered something? I mean really, truly pondered?

3. Every moment with Jesus has meaning, but what *is* that meaning? What is he trying to teach you, today, right this very minute?

4. So much of the real, deep, *good* stuff in life doesn't come packaged with immediate answers. Take, for example, discerning a vocation, choosing a college, living on your own for the first time, starting a new job, getting married, or bringing home a baby. Those things require time, deep thought, lots of prayer, and the potential for mistakes. How does it feel to think about something and not understand it totally right away? How can you turn that feeling into trust in God?

5. Reread Luke 2:18–19. What can we learn from Mary in these passages?

Fiat

Pick one thing that you feel God wants you to ponder more deeply. Spend some time contemplating it with him.

Prayer

Lord, help me keep my mind ever fixed on you, who are all-good and all-loving. Help me, Lord, to follow you, to seek you, to contemplate you. Help me to slip my hand into yours and see you in each moment. Mother Mary, pray for me, that, like you, I too will keep everything in my heart and ponder the puzzle pieces God so generously gives to me. May I one day step back and gasp at the beautiful picture of my life, covered so graciously by God's own fingerprints. Mother, there are so many distractions today, so many things that vie for my attention or promise that they'll satisfy me. There are so many outlets aside from God I can turn to for answers. Please help me enter the discomfort of pondering, so that I can dig deeper until I find the heart—God's heart—in everything. Amen.

FAITH

The Lord's Words Would Be Fulfilled

[And] blessed is she who believed that there would be
a fulfillment of what was spoken to her by the Lord.

—LUKE 1:45

After eight days had passed, it was time to circumcise
the child. . . .

—LUKE 2:21

I walked around for years—*years*—with that little nugget
from Courtney tucked in my back pocket. Deep down, I
knew it was true. I didn't know how God would use me.
I didn't even understand *why* he'd choose me, of all people. But I trusted that, at some point, I'd see those words
unfold before my eyes. After all, if what Courtney said
wasn't of God, why did my heart burst with love of God
as goosebumps leapt to my skin? How could my insides

69

swell and swirl, as though my soul was rising to life within me?

Those weren't regular responses to normal human interactions. Thus, I reasoned, what she said had to be divine. So I believed it.

Until one night.

I paced the room, nursing my infant with a rosary dangling through my fingers. In the sliver of light shining from the closet, I squinted at my beat-up book of Rosary reflections. My mind drifted as my fingers passed bead-by-bead over the decades, the prayers passing my lips in thoughtless whispers.

As I stumbled my way through the meditations, Courtney popped to mind, along with her message to me. For the first time ever, I no longer felt confident in her words. Instead, I felt disappointed. Embarrassed. Angry, even. How could I have believed what she said for so long? How could I be so naïve?

My fingers sped along the beads, but, as I plowed through the Joyful Mysteries with mindless Hail Marys, all I could think about was Courtney.

It had been *years* since she and I had crossed paths, and nothing had happened. No special call from God. Nothing big. Nothing at all, in fact. Wouldn't God have already done something if Courtney's message was true? What if she had gotten the wrong girl? What if she never actually heard those words from God, but just felt like sharing some vague, empowering word with a stranger? What if she was totally nuts? Any of those situations seemed far more possible.

That's it, I fumed silently in the nursery. *Enough of this nonsense. I'm done believing what she said. Clearly it's not true.*

And, with that, I resolutely moved to the next bead on my blessed rosary and turned my attention to the very next reflection in my prayer book:

Blessed is she who believed the Lord's words to her would be fulfilled.

I gasped aloud, not even caring if I woke the baby.

There they were again. The goosebumps. The hum of life inside me. The profound awe of God seated deeply in my soul.

I knew those words were originally meant for Mary, but in that moment, I felt in my bones that they were also meant for me.

For all of us, really.

More often than not, God's words seem fantastical. Impossible, even.

And yet, there's Mary, who had all sorts of words proclaimed over her life. Favored. Full of grace. Blessed. Mother of my Lord. And, as she held her little baby before his circumcision, she may have considered the words that Scripture had already spoken over the coming Messiah. Wonderful Counselor. Mighty God. Eternal Father. Prince of Peace (see Isaiah 9:6).

Surely Mary tucked those nuggets away in a safe corner of her heart to ponder later.

Then, it happened.

The baby was circumcised, officially entering into the eternal covenant between God and his people. The Messiah was here in the flesh, and he was here in the family. They were all united as one. Together with God.

So . . .

Now what?

Jesus was here, all right, but he hardly looked ready to save the world.

Perhaps Mary looked down at her eight-day-old baby, his body so light in her arms, wondering what would come next. When would he do all the things he was supposed to do? Perhaps Jesus gazed back at her, his little eyes heavy with sleep. He was so small, so weak. He couldn't even feed himself, let alone save a multitude of people. How would he hold the whole world in his hands when he couldn't even hold up his own head?

Still, the words proclaimed over her remained. Favored. Full of grace. Blessed. Mother of my Lord.

Mary walked around for years—*years*—with those little nuggets from the angel Gabriel and Elizabeth in her back pocket. Deep down, she knew they were true. She probably didn't know how it would look, this whole mothering the Messiah thing. She probably didn't even understand *why* God had chosen her, of all people.

But she trusted that, at some point, she'd see all those words unfold before her eyes.

As it tends to do sometimes, God's timing dragged out for days, weeks, months, and years. Decades, even.

At any point, Mary could have let doubt creep in, the passage of time eroding her faith. But her trust in God's word never wavered.

Not everyone may bump into an angel or a curbside preacher who prophesies over their life, but God's Word is living and true, and he proclaims things over all of us, every single day:

God made you. (See Psalm 139:13)

You are incredibly valuable. (See Isaiah 43:4)

You are immensely and immeasurably loved. (See John 3:16)

You are good and your life has purpose. (See Ephesians 2:10)

We separate ourselves from God when we choose not to love and obey him (see Romans 6:23), but God sacrificed himself so you could live and be together with him again. (See Romans 5:9–10)

If you stick with him, he will give you eternal life. (See 1 John 2:24–25)

More often than not, these things sound fantastical. Impossible, even.

But blessed is she who believes the Lord's words to her will be fulfilled.

❧ A Soul That Magnifies ❧

Faith

I've thought about my exchange with Courtney countless times. Everything about that moment seems singed in my memory. The way her bright blue eyes misted with emotion. The way she looked at me with hope. The shock I felt at her unanticipated message. The way my body reacted unexpectedly and inexplicably. The way I stood there, unresponsive, trying to process what had just happened.

Then the years of silence. Of nothingness. Of wondering, "What now?"

When the answers didn't come, I allowed doubt to creep in instead.

But not Mary.

Don't get me wrong, Mary still had to wait. God's words to her weren't fulfilled immediately.

On the day she brought Jesus to get him circumcised, she watched her Son enter the covenant of God's people. This baby in her hands was the God who *created* the covenant. And yet, here he was—a tiny, helpless thing—entering the blessed relationship from the side of the people. At that moment, God became both ends of the promise. He was the God who made the promise and part of God's chosen people who entered into it with him. He was the beginning and the end. The God and the human.

But Mary had to wait to find out exactly how God would keep his promise. She had to wait to see if God's words to her would truly be fulfilled. And wait she did, not for a few years, but for three *decades*.

Because faith is long-term trust as God's plan unfolds. It means trusting that God is going to do what he says, even if it takes *thirty years* for it to happen. Mary knew all about that kind of faith. So, undeterred by the delay, she chose to say yes. She chose to believe. She chose to trust.

And for that very reason, all generations will forever call her blessed.

Ponder in Your Heart

1. What is God calling you to trust him with today?

2. What does God say about who you are? What does he say about who he is?

3. How does it feel to give God the hard, messy, confusing parts of your life?

4. Reread Luke 1:45 while imagining God is speaking it over you.

Fiat

What is God saying to you today? Go to Mass or Adoration, or dive into Scripture and ask him. Then listen. How can you show that you believe his word to you is true?

Prayer

You, O Lord, have the words of everlasting life. To whom else would I go? Jesus, please don't ever let me tire of hearing your voice, and help me believe that the words you speak to me are true. Remind me that when I cannot hear you in prayer, I can run to the Scriptures to hear your voice. Your Word, O God, is living. It is true. And though heaven and earth may pass away, your words will never pass away. Mother Mary, pray for me that I may cling to God's promises and believe what he says will be fulfilled. Amen.

RESPONSIBILITY

The Name the Angel Had Given

After eight days had passed, it was time to circumcise
the child; and he was called Jesus, the name given by
the angel before he was conceived in the womb.

—LUKE 2:21

My husband and I have a very particular way of naming
our babies. A way that, as practiced parents, we're
extremely bad at.

You see, we understand that from the moment of
conception, our children are completely new and completely unique individuals. Ones that God knows intimately. He knows who they are and who he wishes for
them to become. He hand-delivered their strengths
and weaknesses, their deep-seated desires, and their
personalities.

So while they're in my womb, we pray desperately
that God will reveal to us who he has made them to be.

Then we name them after saints with similar characteristics so our kids will have role models to relate to and admire throughout their whole lives. Because, to us, a name is more than simply a name. A name can declare one's God-given identity.

It wasn't a surprise, then, that while I was pregnant with our second child, my husband and I sat on the bed praying over her. In that moment, God placed it on our hearts that she would be bold and fierce. A trailblazer for God. Like St. Elizabeth Ann Seton. Yeah. That sounded good. My husband and I nodded along to that idea. The world could use a little pumping up for Jesus.

So we named her Elizabeth Ann.

What we failed to realize, however, was that our fearless, bold, trailblazing baby would also be two years old, and three years old, and four years old. And by golly, it's traumatizing to *raise* a trailblazer.

Every day was saturated with screaming and tears and tantrums. And, every day, a good chunk of my sanity shriveled up and died.

At night, as my precious daughter shrieked from behind the bars of her crib, I questioned whether I could undertake such a calling.

How can I possibly lead a fearless trailblazer?

How can I possibly teach the faith to someone who only does things her way?

How can I possibly be this person's mother?!

My sweet, wonderful, boldly fierce girl definitely lives up to her name, that's for sure. So much so, we've been paralyzed in fear while trying to name the rest of our children. There's a weighty responsibility attached to naming a child that we hadn't fully understood until that point. So, with every subsequent kid, we cautiously approached God in prayer about who they were to become.

"Please God, pleeeeease"—I've squeezed my eyes shut, fingers clenched in prayer—"who's the patron saint of sleep? Or silence? Can we name this next baby after them?"

Though God hasn't given us any silent babies or sleepers, he has come through in the clutch and been spot on with all five of our children. (Go figure.) He has known all my kids to their cores before we even knew their faces. And as they all live and grow, they seem to mature into the identity that rests in their name.

How weighty it must've been for Mary, then, when the angel said her baby's name would be Jesus. A name that literally means "God saves." Sheesh, "God saves" seems even harder to parent than "trailblazer."

I wonder if Mary realized that her world-saving Son would also be two years old, and three years old, and four years old. And by golly, I can't imagine how much responsibility it would take to raise the God who saves.

Perhaps, like me, she questioned what it would look like to undertake such a calling.

How can I lead the God who saves?

How can I teach the Faith to the One who created it?

How can I possibly live up to the call of being this Person's Mother?

But she didn't shrink from the weight of her responsibility. Every time Mary called her Son's name, she boldly proclaimed who he is. God saves.

And boy, Jesus definitely lived up to his name.

⚜ A Soul That Magnifies ⚜

Responsibility

Responsibility. Ugh. It's such a dry word—so jam-packed with serious adultness—that it can leave a bitter taste in one's mouth. Responsibilities aren't exciting. Nobody seeks them out. Nobody wants *more* of them—most people don't want any at all. More often than not, there are temptations to skirt responsibilities: to *say* we'll do something, and then, at the last second, bail.

I've seen it time and again. Heck, I've felt those temptations myself.

But Mary? She had a different approach to responsibility. When she committed to something, she truly committed to it, no matter what—be it her promise to give her Son that significantly profound name spoken by the angel or her agreement to be the Mother of God.

Think about that. The Mother of God.

That may very well be the weightiest responsibility in the history of humanity. There were no others like her. No mentors to mimic. No other mothers she could turn to and ask, "I'm having trouble figuring out how to such-and-such. How did you handle that when *you* raised God?"

And yet, Mary agreed to it. She said yes. She hoisted the weight of her responsibility onto her shoulders and carried it her whole life. She showed up. Every single day. I'm sure there were days she was tired. I bet there were days she was confused, fearful, or feeling inadequate. Perhaps there were days she wanted to phone it in.

But she had given her word. And her word meant something.

When she said she'd do something, by golly, it got done. She held herself accountable. To her, the word "responsibility" may have sounded less like a burdensome cross and more like an honorable duty.

With that level of dependability, she probably didn't go around making promises willy-nilly. Because when we say "yes" to one thing, we're essentially saying "no" to everything else. So Mary was probably wise about *what* she committed herself to. She made sure her "yes" meant "yes" and her "no" meant "no."

Then, out of love, she upheld all her responsibilities.

Ponder in Your Heart

1. What responsibilities has God given to you today? How can you lovingly accept those responsibilities and hold yourself accountable to take care of them? How can you "show up" today?

2. How often does your "yes" mean "yes" and "no" mean "no"? How can you discern which responsibilities you choose to undertake?

3. Reread Luke 2:21. Because Mary followed through with the responsibility of naming her Son Jesus—the name he had been given before he was even conceived—you and I can know God by name. What do you think God wants us to know about who he is through the gift of his name?

Fiat

When you give someone your word, uphold it. Let your "yes" mean "yes" and your "no" mean "no."

Prayer

Jesus, you have said that if we have seen you, we have seen the Father. Your name alone reveals God's identity, his character. You, Jesus, are the God who saves. How is it possible that you give yourself to me so intimately? That the Creator of the cosmos wants me to know him by name? Mary, what must it have been like to gaze upon your Son's face and see Salvation itself? Pray for me, Holy Mother, that, like you, I may be reliable in word and deed. That I will lovingly uphold the responsibilities God gives me. Even when I'm tired or scared or feeling inadequate. Even when I just don't feel like doing it. Help me carry the weight of my "yeses," and give me the wisdom and strength to say "no" when I must. Amen.

GENEROSITY

The Presentation

> When the time came for their purification according to the law of Moses, they brought him up to Jerusalem to present him to the Lord.
>
> —LUKE 2:22

Typically, kids cling to their treasures, desperately trying to hoard them all to themselves. The thought of *not* having their things—of losing them or giving them away—comes with great pain as panic churns in their little hearts.

But strangely, that panicked feeling seems to vanish when they give stuff to their mother. Maybe it's because they know their mother is a good teammate. Someone who's got their best interests at heart.

Because of that, kids have a beautiful way of giving gifts to their mothers.

So it wasn't too surprising when my three-year-old recently approached me and gingerly extended a closed fist. Inside, no doubt, was something special. He always lavishes me with his most prized possessions. Sticks. Pieces of trash. Whatever he finds to be of note becomes a gift for his mother to safeguard.

With it, the three-year-old offered a little bow. "I present this to you, Mom," he said in his most regal voice.

"You *present* this to me?" I touched my heart in genuine wonderment.

I reached out my hand. One by one, two dirty, brown rocks plopped into my hand.

"I don't want you to ever get sad, so I give those to you to be happy," he said, beaming from ear to ear.

I feigned a gasp and wrapped my fingers around my newest treasures. "I will cherish these forever."

Satisfied, he nodded in triumph and then ran back to playing at the park.

I stared at the gifts in my hand, and though the rocks left dirt in my palm, a smile spread across my face. Something about these rocks was special. To my son, at least. But the meaning behind the gesture? *That* was truly worthwhile.

I love you, my son was saying. *I love you so much that I want to give you the very best I have to offer. I love you so much, I want to be someone who brings a smile to your face.*

Because the dirty, old rocks were special to him—the little boy whom I love more than the entire world—they were special to me. But what was I going to do with a couple of dirty rocks? I knew they'd "accidentally" get lost somewhere.

But it got me thinking: What do I give my Mother Mary?

Typically, I cling to my treasures, desperately trying to hoard them all to myself. The thought of *not* having my things—of losing them or giving them away—comes with great pain as panic churns in my heart.

But strangely, that panicked feeling tends to vanish when I give stuff to my Mother. Maybe it's because I know my Mother is a good teammate. Someone who's got my best interests at heart.

So it wasn't too surprising when I received a gentle tug to consecrate myself to Mary and promise to walk hand-in-hand with her as I pursued Jesus. After all, Mary is really good at giving everything she has to God. There is absolutely nothing she hoards for herself. We learn that in the Presentation.

I mean, the birth of Jesus was a bit surreal, to be sure. Even though Mary and Joseph had nine months to wait and prepare for him, Jesus was also the Messiah their people had been waiting for—*longing* for—for *centuries*. So much history, turmoil, strife, and hope had built them up to this point. And now God was finally there with them. Emmanuel. What more could they have ever dreamed of? What else could they have hoped to hold in their hands besides their God in the flesh? And yet, instead of hoarding him for themselves, they obediently and rightfully brought him to the Temple to present him to God.

Be it a small gift or a big one, Mary gives everything she has to God.

It makes sense, then, to think she'd do the same with me if I willingly put myself in her hands.

Gingerly, I extended a closed fist. I wasn't an expert at lavishing gifts by any means, but this time I grasped the smooth beads of a blessed rosary. That seemed like something worthy enough to be a gift for my Mother.

"All right, Mary," my voice quivered with uncertainty. "With this rosary, I offer my heart to you."

"You offer this to me?" I imagine she replied, touching her heart in genuine wonderment.

I reached out my hands and began praying, my fingers slowly grazing over each smooth bead. One by one, my two sin-stained hands grazed the beads until all fifty-three Hail Marys were completed. Finally, I plopped my heart into her hands.

"I don't want you to ever get sad, so I give myself to you to be happy," I said childishly.

"Wow." I imagine she gasped, gently receiving her newest treasure. "I will cherish this forever."

Satisfied, I nodded in triumph and then ran back to my life in this world.

Perhaps she stared at the gift in her hand, and though the sinfulness of my heart surely left dirt in her palm, a smile spread across her face. This heart was special. To her Son, at least. But the meaning behind the gesture? That was truly worthwhile.

Mary, I love you and your Son. I love you both so much, I want to give you the very best I have to offer. I love you so much, I want to be someone who brings a smile to your faces.

Because my sinful heart was special to Jesus—the little boy whom Mary loved more than the entire world—it was special to her, too. But what was Mary going to do with my heart? I knew it would never "accidentally" get lost somewhere. No doubt, Mary would tuck it safely into her mantle and make good on her promise to protect such a treasure.

She does that the best way she knows how. She brings it directly to God.

❧ A Soul That Magnifies ❧

Generosity

Mary's first inclination is to give everything she has to God, even her very own beloved Son. Through obedience to Jewish law, she brought Jesus to the Temple at the appointed time to consecrate him. Everything that Mary received—be it a kind word or the Word Itself—she immediately gave back to God.

To her, generosity wasn't a "giving up" but a "giving *to*," since it always involves sharing with another. With generosity, there is always a recipient. And, out of love, Mary gave her all, no strings attached. She didn't worry if there'd be enough left over for her. She didn't obsess about getting her things back. She simply gave. Her time, her thoughts, her things, her prayers. Everything. The entirety of her life was spent generously—giving it as a gift to God and enriching those around her.

Following her example, we, too, can live generously. Be it big or small. A spiritual gift or a physical one. Our time, our thoughts, our things, our prayers. Everything. Like Mary, we can give the entirety of our lives *for* God and *to* God, including living generously with other people because we know how immensely God loves them.

Ponder in Your Heart

1. What are some things in your life that you cling to? How does it feel to think about not having them?

2. How can you let them go and trust Christ to fulfill your needs?

3. Read Luke 2:22–24. What does this say about what Mary does with her most cherished possessions?

4. What would Mary do with you if you gave yourself to her?

Fiat

Give your heart to Mary, trusting she will bring you closer to God. Then, knowing how much God loves the people in your life, give something of yours to someone else.

Prayer

Jesus, I want my life to bring a smile to your face. When you think of me, I hope you delight in your creation. Each day, I long to give you the very best I have to offer, but on my own I grow weak. On my own, I wander off track. I get confused and weary. Thank you for giving me a wonderful Mother who will pick me up when I fall and lead me down the narrow path that leads to you. Mary, I don't have much to offer you. All I have is my fickle, sin-stained heart, but I give it to you nonetheless. Please take me as I am—all of me—and return me to the Father, as you did with baby Jesus. You, who turn everything into praise of God, take me and transform my heart into a gift that delights him. I reach out to you now, Mary, the way a little child reaches for her mother. Please take my hand and lead me to your Son. Amen.

REDEMPTIVE SUFFERING

Simeon's Prophecy

Guided by the Spirit, Simeon came into the temple; and when the parents brought in the child Jesus, to do for him what was customary under the law . . . Simeon blessed them and said to his mother Mary, "This child is destined for the falling and the rising of many in Israel, and to be a sign that will be opposed so that the inner thoughts of many will be revealed—and a sword will pierce your own soul too."

—LUKE 2:27, 34–35

Writhing.

That's how I rang in the new year. While the rest of the world was celebrating, kissing, and attacking their resolutions with fresh fervor, I lay writhing in bed with a fever. My temperature spiked dangerously high, which was strange because my bones felt frozen. My head pounded. Everything hurt. Even my eyeballs felt bruised. The simple rise and fall of my chest sent searing pain through my body. The sheer act of living hurt.

My natural instinct when it comes to pain is to fight it. Resist it. So, I clenched my jaw and steeled myself against the chills, which only made them worse.

The minutes crawled, as though time itself were in as much pain as I was. How long had I been thrashing here beneath this mountain of blankets? How many times could my teeth chatter in the span of one minute? Hundreds? Thousands? Was that the easiest way to track time now?

The sun shone through my bedroom window, taunting me with its cheeriness. I groaned and willed myself to roll over, daring a peek at the clock.

11:11.

My heart smiled. According to my kids, you can make a wish at that time. I squeezed my eyes shut as the pain raged in my head.

If I had one wish, what would it be?

I fought through my delirious, fever-riddled mind for an answer. One wish. Better make it good.

But there was only one thing I really wanted. "I wish we could go back to last year," I croaked out loud to myself.

Nothing happened, of course. I stayed, stuck, writhing and wriggling in the same bed, in the same year.

Just like that, the wishing away of my own suffering fell flat on my lips and died. Because sometimes suffering is unavoidable. Suffering doesn't care a single thing about my wishes and wants. It stays as long as it likes, regardless of how I feel about it. There's no reasoning—no bargaining—with suffering.

With suffering, sometimes there's only enduring. Mary knew that. The lady was an expert at suffering because God prepared her from the start to handle her hardships with trust, uniting her sacrifice to that of her Son. By prayerfully pondering Simeon's words that her Son would be opposed and a sword would pierce her soul, Mary came to understand and accept that the trials she would face were a part of God's plan. This let her face the difficult future bravely, with confidence that God would use whatever suffering came for his plan of salvation.

For that reason, Mary never wished away the pain or fearfully waited for the proverbial axe to fall, stabbing her straight in the soul. Neither did she cast off her cross once it was hers to bear.

Not even after Simeon prophesied over her, detailing the painful future she was doomed to endure.

Not even when a ruthless ruler demanded the death of her Son and sent her fleeing to a foreign country.

Not even when she lost the child Jesus and had no idea where to find him for three whole days.

Not even when Joseph died, making her a single mother and widow in a patriarchal society and leaving her all alone as the only person in the world raising the Son of God.

Not even when she stood at the foot of the cross, gaping up at her Son as his blood poured down the pole and pooled on the ground.

Not even when death greedily slurped up Jesus' last bits of breath, cuing the Roman soldiers to finally take him off that God-forsaken cross.

Mary knew all about suffering, but instead of wishing it away, she courageously endured her pain *with* Jesus and *for* Jesus. After all, Mary knew what God was capable of—she knew at any point Jesus could have freed himself from the cross. He could have escaped. But he didn't. He chose to endure the suffering, for love's sake. By staying on the cross, Jesus did something more heroic than fighting it. He used his cross to save us. He took the ugliness of suffering and transformed it into the glory of salvation.

But Jesus didn't suffer alone.

Mary was there too, trusting Jesus, accompanying him on that journey, and suffering with him.

All at once, the hazy cloud in my fevered mind parted, and my approach changed. I would not fight my *suffering*. I'd fight the ugliness of the world *with* my suffering. I'd surrender it over to God so that he could convert it into a force for salvation.

Jesus, if you wish that I suffer now, I choose to suffer with you.

Jesus, take my fever and chills, and use them.

Jesus, take this pounding in my head and use it.

Jesus, take my achy body and use it.

Jesus, I trust in you.

All of a sudden, my malady had meaning. It was no longer a cross to fight. A cross to resist. No, this was a cross to be embraced. A cross to be *used*.

So I clenched my jaw and steeled myself, ready to endure my suffering and wield it as a deadly weapon against evil by giving it to Jesus as an offering for others.

❧ A Soul That Magnifies ❧

Redemptive Suffering

Let's be real: there's a lot of suffering in this world right now. I bet you have suffering in your life, be it physical, emotional, or spiritual. We all do.

Typically, I worry about suffering before it even comes into my life. Then, when it rears its ugly head, I try to fight it, tooth and nail.

Mary, on the other hand, shows us how to handle suffering in a healthier, more fruitful and faithful way. During the times when there was nothing she could do to assuage the pain, Mary endured her suffering and united it to God's mission, offering it up for the salvation of the world.

There's something about suffering that makes it hard to see. Hard to remember that life exists outside of your own little bubble. When we're in the state of suffering, all we can see is our own pain. But what if our pain could be used as the salve for someone else's? What if our pain could be a prompt to think of and pray for someone else instead of staying hyper-focused on ourselves? What would happen if we stopped fighting our suffering, but instead willingly endured and gave it to Jesus?

Mary chose to do that her whole life, especially at the foot of the cross. On that awful Friday, she didn't fight the Roman soldiers or try to knock the cross down. Those things would've only made matters worse and, most likely, caused more people to suffer. There was nothing she could do to alleviate this pain. All she could do was endure it. How? In the moments of her most unbearable suffering, Mary stayed close to Jesus and kept her eyes fixed on him.

Ponder in Your Heart

1. How do you normally respond to pain and hardship in your life? What difficulties do you have right now?

2. How can you suffer with Jesus and for Jesus? How can you offer your suffering to God on behalf of someone else?

3. Reread Luke 2:34–35. Mary has a knack for keeping her eyes on the prize. The prize being Jesus, of course. She's there at the passion. She's there at the Cross. She's there at Jesus' burial. In the worst of the worst moments, she's there, keeping her eyes on Jesus. How can you keep your eyes on Jesus during your most difficult moments?

Fiat

Give Jesus whatever suffering you have in your life and ask him to use it for good.

Prayer

Lord, you see how I suffer. You feel the weight of my cross because you are here carrying it with me. When my body writhes with illness or injury, take my suffering and use it. When my spirit writhes with longing for you, Lord, take my suffering and use it. When my mind and emotions turn in turmoil within me, let me offer them to you. When I have done all I can to alleviate my suffering but it still remains, show me how to endure it and give it to you. Please don't let even one drop of my pain go to waste, but instead transform it all into something good, the same way you did on the cross. Help me be more like Mary, who never shrank from the call to suffer, but instead endured it with you. For you and your will. For all of us, really, so we could experience the glory of what came next. Amen.

COURAGE

Fleeing to Egypt

Now after they had left, an angel of the Lord appeared to Joseph in a dream and said, "Get up, take the child and his mother, and flee to Egypt, and remain there until I tell you; for Herod is about to search for the child, to destroy him." Then Joseph got up, took the child and his mother by night, and went to Egypt.

—Matthew 2:13–14

Summer in Texas is my worst nightmare. The blazing heat brings out all the brightly colored bugs, armed with slick exoskeletons, sharp stingers, and vendettas against humans. Surely, they all come straight from the devil.

As a mom, however, I'm supposed to be the brave one. The one who calmly shoos the bugs away. The one my kids can run to when *they* are scared. But it's been hard for my kids to find refuge in my arms because I'm constantly flinching, flailing, and sprinting away from all the stinging things.

Until one day when a yellow jacket landed on my daughter's back. Slowly, curiously, it started crawling up toward her neck.

Gulp.

You're the mom, I silently prodded myself, *you've got to do something!*

"Baby," the word stretched and trembled across my lips, "don't move."

Don't move? Funny advice from the lady who *should* have been moving but wasn't. I couldn't. Sweat dripped from my temple as I tried to push away the childhood memory of stepping on a hornets' nest. The screams. The pain. The unexpected hum of hundreds of wings. The desperate fleeing in fear.

Even now, as I stared at this lone yellow jacket, I could practically feel the fiery burn of stingers searing my skin.

Slowly, I grabbed a plastic baseball bat that was lying in the grass and hesitantly flicked it at the insect. The bug didn't even flinch. If anything, it climbed toward my daughter's hair with more determination.

Panic rose inside as I realized with dread what needed to be done. I released the bat and let it drop lazily to my feet.

I took a step forward. *What if this plan fails and I make this demon-bug really mad?*

Another step. *I'll have to make sure my kids make it inside, even if it starts stinging me.*

One last step and I was pretty much face-to-face with the monster. A shiver ran down my spine. *Gosh, those things are ugly.*

I raised an open palm. My daughter cringed, realizing what was going to happen.

I lifted my hand into the air—*slowly, slowly*—scrutinizing every step the bug took with all six of its nasty, yellow legs. Until . . .

I swung quickly, making contact with its sleek, hard-shelled body, swiping it off my daughter's shoulder blade. In a daze, the bug fell and flew away.

I breathed a sigh of relief. None of the kids were harmed. My job, at least for the moment, was finished.

In a much more profound way, that's exactly what Mary did for Jesus.

You see, the moment the angel Gabriel left Mary alone with the words of his Annunciation, she was the Mother now. Her arms were to be the refuge. And if anything scared her, she had to gulp down her fear to protect her child. She had to be courageous for the sake of her Son.

And when Satan lashed out, his nasty tongue making a decree to kill all baby boys under two years old, Mary courageously protected her baby.

Sweat may have dripped from Mary's temple as memories of Moses filled her mind, along with the decree from Pharaoh demanding the mass execution of Jewish baby boys. The screams. The pain. The unexpected hum of hundreds of armed soldiers ransacking the town. The desperate fleeing in fear.

So as Mary listened to Joseph recount what the angel had told him, she knew she'd have to do something to protect Jesus. But how could a teenaged girl like her protect the great I AM? Like Jochebed, would she have to set Jesus adrift in a basket somewhere?

Panic may have risen inside her as she realized with dread that they'd need to leave everything behind—including those beautiful gifts from the Magi—and flee before Herod's men could find them.

Maybe with Joseph's hand in hers, she found the courage to take the first step forward into the blackness of night. *What if this plan fails and we make Herod really mad? What if he has someone follow us? What if he tracks us down?*

Another step, cloaked in secrecy. *What will my parents think when they hear about this decree, and Joseph and I don't return home?*

One last step. Surely her heart ached, heavy in her chest, knowing the devastation that was to befall Bethlehem. *I'll have to make sure Jesus makes it someplace safe, even if it kills me.*

As they crisscrossed through town, Mary may have lifted the folds of her cloak to conceal her baby. Maybe they crept along the outskirts of the city, shushing in the baby's ear—*slowly, slowly*—trying to hide in the shadows as they left behind everything and everyone they knew.

Onward, they courageously stepped into their new lives as refugees in a strange new land. Penniless. Jobless. Unable to speak the language. In a country that had once enslaved their ancestors, they had to some-how take root.

Yet, as they crossed the border into Egypt, I imagine they breathed a sigh of relief.

The baby wasn't harmed. Mary's job, at least for the moment, was finished.

❧ A Soul That Magnifies ❧

Courage

Because of their strength and intense love for their children, mothers are fierce protectors.

I've heard of women finding the strength to lift a car because their kid was trapped underneath it.

I've heard of women fighting off wild animals with their bare hands to protect their child.

I've heard of women running into fire and jumping in front of bullets and using their bodies to shield others from natural disasters.

All for the sake of their child.

Because that's what love does—not just for moms, but for all of us. It makes us bolder, stronger, able to do things we never thought possible.

That is exactly what Mary does for us. Her hand doesn't just swat away tiny (albeit terrifying) bugs. Instead, her heel forever crushes the head of the serpent. She doesn't hesitantly shoo away yellow jackets. No, she jumps full force into the raging spiritual war to protect her children from the sting of Satan's bite.

That fierce, ferocious, momma-bear kind of love is exactly what Mary offers to you.

Mary isn't a passive, disinterested mother. She's courageous. She proved that by doing some pretty intense stuff to protect her Son. Then, when Jesus bequeathed her to us from the Cross, you became her baby. And by golly, that Mother will do anything to protect her babies.

But we don't have to be a biological mother to employ heroic acts of courage. You see, when we allow ourselves to be enfolded in Mary's shroud, she courageously protects us from the Enemy who tries to snatch and sting us. Then, aided by her example and motherly protection, we too can reach out and courageously protect others in need.

That doesn't necessarily mean we have to lift cars or fight bears—thank heavens! We can live courageously simply by going against the grain to stand up for what's right, or accompanying someone through a dark time, or speaking up when we see a loved one falling into a harmful habit. Following Mary's example, we can find ways to be courageous for Jesus—and our neighbors—every day.

Ponder in Your Heart

1. What does courage look like, both in the big things and in the smaller, everyday things?

2. We can't be brave if we're not a little scared first. Is there anything that makes you a little scared? How can you be courageous in those areas of your life?

3. Reread Matthew 2:13–14. Put yourself in Mary's shoes and imagine how scary that situation must have been. And yet, perfect love casts out fear. For Mary and Joseph, their love for Jesus (and their desire to protect him) was bigger than their fear, which helped them choose courage when the time came. How can you show that your love for Jesus is bigger than your fears?

Fiat

Think of a situation where you're tempted to choose fear, and instead choose to respond courageously.

Prayer

God, you are all-powerful and almighty. With all your power and all your might, you could have literally done anything, and you chose to make me. Not just to make me, but to make me in your image and likeness. To give me a spirit not of fear, but of power, and of love, and of self-control. God, I pray that when the time for courage comes, you will be my strength. Help me love you above all, so that my big love for you may cast out any fears. Mary, through God's grace, I wish to be courageous like you. Mother, I love getting to be your child. Help me find safety and refuge in your arms. Protect and defend me so that I may also rise up and courageously protect those in need. Amen.

PERSEVERANCE

The Return to Jerusalem to Look for Jesus

Now every year his parents went to Jerusalem for the festival of the Passover. And when he was twelve years old, they went up as usual for the festival. When the festival was ended and they started to return, the boy Jesus stayed behind in Jerusalem, but his parents did not know it. Assuming that he was in the group of travelers, they went a day's journey. Then they started to look for him among their relatives and friends. When they did not find him, they returned to Jerusalem to search for him. After three days they found him in the temple, sitting among the teachers, listening to them and asking them questions. And all who heard him were amazed at his understanding and his answers.

—Luke 2:41–47

My parents were in town and decided to treat us to lunch at Dave & Busters. Of course, "lunch" merely meant an hour of grabbing my kids' wandering attention and repeating the phrase, "We can play games after you eat."

Eventually, everyone finished their meals. It was time to play.

I grabbed the stroller where my infant son slept and slowly steered our whole crew toward the desk to get a game card. Coins rained down beside us. Someone must've won something big.

"We'll take turns picking the games," I shouted above the noise, then handed the card to our three-year-old. "You can pick first."

She ran through the aisles, racing by on two stubby legs and sizing up each game in a blink. Finally, she settled on one, swiped the card, and whacked away at a blinking button. She couldn't have cared less about the rules. She was entranced by the flashing lights and her favorite characters that hopped along each time she slapped the button.

Almost as soon as it started, it was over. I passed the card to my five-year-old. "Okay," I said, as loudly as I could. "Your turn to pick a game."

In a flash, we were off again, following the more deliberate path of my oldest daughter. She, too, wound through every aisle, and I followed behind, steering the stroller through small spaces to keep up.

Finally, she made her choice. She swiped the card. She whacked away a few times. And, again, the game was over.

At this rate, we'd blow through the whole game card in ten minutes. It was the three-year-old's turn again. I turned to hand her the card.

But she wasn't there.

I glanced around at the games nearby. Nothing.

"Where's Elizabeth?" my mom shouted, her eyes wide with panic.

I called for my daughter. Shouted her name over and over.

But the music and the noise and the dinging machines were too loud. I couldn't even hear myself. How on earth would my toddler hear me?

Heart pounding in my chest, I zigzagged through the video games. Could she be hiding in the photo booth? What about in one of those racecar games? What if she had wandered out the front door looking for us? What if she toddled into the street??

I darted toward the front doors, squeezing and swerving between games. The noise was dizzying, the music now ominous. Every game was just another hidey hole where my daughter could be but wasn't. Everything about the place merely added to the terrifying fact that I could not find my daughter.

But I wouldn't stop. Couldn't stop.

I. Would. Find. Her. If it was the last thing I did.

I turned the last corner before the big opening of the front archway, and there, with tears streaming down her face, was my three-year-old.

I rushed to her and scooped her into my arms. Suddenly, everything around us seemed to quiet. All I could hear was her sweet, scared little voice. "I couldn't find you, Mommy," she hiccupped in my ear. "I didn't know you left."

I had no words, so I squeezed her tight until her tears dried on my shoulder.

My daughter had only been gone a few minutes, and it felt like an eternity. I can't imagine what three *days* must've felt like for Mary.

There they were, walking into the city, eyes wide, taking in the glory that was Jerusalem. This place bustled with excitement. Laughter. Shouts and songs of praise to God.

Then, all too soon, it was time to go home. Slowly, they would've steered their whole crew toward Nazareth. When they settled down to camp for the night, Mary may have scoured the crowd for her Son.

But he wasn't there.

Surely, she glanced around at the families nearby. Nothing.

"Where's Jesus?" someone may have asked. Heck, *she* may have asked that question, eyes wide with panic.

Surely, in that instance, she would have called for her Son. Shouted his name over and over.

But the singing and the noise and the people may have been too loud.

Perhaps her heart hammered in her chest as she zig-zagged through the crowd. Could he be with other family members? In someone's tent? What if he had wandered away looking for her and Joseph and gotten lost?

Together with Joseph, she darted back toward the gates of Jerusalem, squeezing and swerving between the stragglers. The panic may have been dizzying. Every home was just another hidey hole where her Son could be but wasn't. Everything about the place merely added to the terrifying fact that she could not find her Son.

But she wouldn't stop. Couldn't stop.

She. Would. Find. Him. If it was the last thing she did.

On the third day, she must've turned into the Temple—whether to search for Jesus or pray for him, I don't know—and there, in the midst of the most learned teachers, was her twelve-year-old.

I imagine her momma's heart propelled her to rush over and wrap her arms around him. Perhaps everything around them seemed to quiet. Then came the voice of her beloved Son. Her Savior. Her God Incarnate. "Why were you searching for me?" he asked. "Did you not know that I must be in my Father's house?"

❦ A Soul That Magnifies ❦

Perseverance

Jesus was sitting among the rabbis—the most learned men in Jewish culture—and confounding them with his wisdom. It makes one wonder if he could really be so wise with the teachers and yet so blatantly oblivious with his own Mother.

I don't think so.

Like always, Jesus had a knack for asking questions, not so *he* could get the answer, but so that the person he was talking to could get the answer.

Why was Mary searching for him? Well, because she loved him so fiercely that she'd persevere through anything to be with him. Eventually, she would prove that at the foot of the Cross.

But when he posed that question, it wasn't just for Mary. It's also for you. For me. For all of us.

Why do we search for him?

Hopefully, like Mary, it's because we love him so fiercely, we'd persevere through anything to be with him. And, hopefully, also like Mary, we can prove that with our lives. We can persevere through spiritual droughts when he seems to have vanished. We can persevere in prayer when he seems silent. We can persevere in getting to Mass, Confession, and Adoration, even when our lives are hectic.

Because, in his infinite goodness, Jesus tells us where we can go to find him. We must simply go to his Father's house. For Mary, that meant the Temple. For us, it's any tabernacle across the globe. There, he always waits for us with open arms.

Then, refilled and refueled by his love, we can find the strength to keep persevering.

Ponder in Your Heart

1. Are you someone who finishes what you start? Or do you find it difficult to see things through to the end?

2. What is important enough to persevere through adversity for?

3. Reread Luke 2:41–47 and put yourself in Mary's shoes. What do you think it may have felt like to lose Jesus? To search desperately for him? To find him?

Fiat

Go to your local church and find Jesus there, waiting for you in the tabernacle.

Prayer

Jesus, you are so good and so faithful. Thank you for always being here for me and being here with me. Lord, give me a heart that seeks you with zealous fervor. Never tiring. Never stopping until I've finally found you. When you feel far away—when I feel as though I've lost you—remind me I can run to find you in your Father's house. There, you wait for me with open arms. Mary, pray for me, that I may pursue your Son because of my great love for him. May I persevere through spiritual deserts until that glorious, joyous day when I find him again. Amen.

PATIENCE

Finding Jesus in the Temple

When his parents saw him they were astonished; and his mother said to him, "Child, why have you treated us like this? Look, your father and I have been searching for you in great anxiety." He said to them, "Why were you searching for me? Did you not know that I must be in my Father's house?" But they did not understand what he said to them. Then he went down with them and came to Nazareth, and was obedient to them. His mother treasured all these things in her heart.

—LUKE 2:48–51

"MOOOOOMMY, WHERE AAAAARE YOUUUU?"

That's what I hear every morning at 6:55 AM.

You see, my three-year-old son only knows two times of day: red and green.

The clock on his dresser across from his bed stands tall, his very own streetlight in his bedroom. At night, it glows red, and my son understands that when the light is red, he needs to be in bed.

Yet, every morning like clockwork, at 6:55 AM the light gloriously switches to green. And green means go. Go out of your bed. Go start the day. Go, go, go until that light turns red again.

I'm pretty sure my son wakes early every morning and stays in his room, his eyes trained on the glowing light. Watching. Waiting. Refusing to blink lest he miss the exact moment when the colors change.

Because every morning at exactly 6:55 AM, he calls me from his room, and I go hug and cuddle him.

But the other day, that didn't happen.

Instead of one voice, I heard all three of my big kids. And they weren't calling out for me to start the day. They were laughing, giggling, and playing together.

At 5:30.

When the light was *so* red.

I marched upstairs, anger growing hot in my cheeks. *My son has always been such a good listener. So obedient. If my daughters have tainted him, have taught him to disobey . . .* oooh, ugly, heated words forced their way into my mouth, but I clenched my teeth to lock them in and barged into my daughters' room.

There, on the floor, all three kids sat, playing beneath heaps of blankets they had stripped off their beds.

All laughter stopped immediately when Mom burst onto the scene.

"What are you guys doing?! It's 5:30 in the morning! No one should be awake right now!" I shot an extra angry glare at my girls, who have a knack for rising early. "If your brother is out of his bed right now, that must mean you were being far too loud!"

Despite the lashing I gave with my words, my oldest daughter looked up at me calmly. Serenely. Maturely. All the things I was not.

"He was crying on the toilet," she said, "so we helped him."

Heat rose into my cheeks again, this time in remorse. Here I had accused my girls of hurting their brother—had even expected they taught him to disobey—and all the while, they'd gone out of their way to be kind to him. To sacrifice their own sleep to take care of him. To be really great big sisters.

I put my ashamed face in my palm. "I'm sorry, guys. Thanks for taking care of your brother."

"You're welcome!" they chirped angelically, and then returned to their play.

As I walked back down the steps, hearing their laughter behind me, I couldn't help but think about Mary.

No doubt, Mary and Joseph drilled twelve-year-old Jesus about their travel plans when it was time to return home from their trip to Jerusalem. Jesus most likely knew when the family was going to leave, and understood what he'd need to bring and what he'd need to do to make it to the next destination. His parents probably even helped him pack the night before so he'd be ready when it was time to leave.

Which means Jesus *chose* to stay behind.

As in, a conscious, deliberate choice.

Now, I don't know about you, but if my kid ever chose to stay behind without telling me, my quotes would have to be written in all caps with lots of symbols and exclamation points.

But not Mary. Mary always puts love before anger and patient understanding before rash judgement.

So, when pre-teen Jesus disappeared for three days, she could have chosen to march back to Jerusalem with anger growing hot in her cheeks. *My son has always been such a good listener. So obedient. If the world has tainted him, has taught him to disobey . . .* oooh, ugly, heated words could've forced their way into her mouth as she barged back through the city gates.

But that's not what happened.

Over the three days of painstaking, panicked searching, she didn't store up angry words to hurl at him. She didn't rush to any false conclusions about why he did what he did. She didn't verbally assault him for going missing.

No, instead, after three days of worry, of endless, exhausting searching, of never giving up on the hope of finding her Son, the first thing she did when she finally found him was ask a simple question.

Why did you do this?

Even when it seemed like there could be no good explanation, she gave Jesus the chance to explain. Even when everything seemed completely incomprehensible, she gave herself the chance to patiently understand. But she didn't understand. Not right away, at least. So she needed even *more* patience to accept that it would take time to grasp why he did what he did, and how it would all make sense in the bigger picture of God's plan.

With that one question, Mary was able to toss out any assumptions, any anger, and genuinely open her heart to Jesus. Because of that—because of her patience—she could approach her Son with love and seek to be together with him again. And then, instead of walking away in remorse, she could walk with love, hand-in-hand with Jesus all the way back home.

⚜ A Soul That Magnifies ⚜

Patience

I always thought I was a patient person.

And then I had kids.

Since then, it has become extremely clear that I lack patience completely. But, like any good skill, it can be developed through practice (and boy, my kids give me *lots* of opportunities to do that).

Practicing virtue—and patience, in particular—can physically hurt, deep down in the core of my spirit. From the depths of my being, my soul cringes and winces, wriggling with discomfort. If you're anything like me, you want to run away from that squirmy feeling and pluck the thorn from your side as soon as possible. But the longer we allow ourselves to sit in those moments and choose to be patient through them, the stronger our souls become.

My kids and I call it "spiritual weightlifting." When we lift weights with our bodies, it can be unpleasant. It can even hurt. But our bodies get stronger because of it.

In the same way, our souls get stronger when we work hard to choose patience whenever we feel annoyed, frustrated, or hurt. So, like Paul with the thorn in his side, we can rejoice and be grateful for all those unpleasant situations in our lives because they help strengthen our spirit.

Despite the fact that Mary was sinless, she still would have felt that squiggly, squirmy, wince-worthy feeling. She still would have struggled with those thorns in her side. And, like us, she still had to make her own choice.

Lift those spiritual weights or let them drop? Be patient or stop waiting? Hold her tongue or let it lash out?

Because of God's grace and all the spiritual weight-lifting that lady did, Mary's soul was in tip-top shape. Ours can be as well, if we let that squirminess sanctify us. With God's help, we too can choose to embrace those thorns in our sides to grow in patience.

Ponder in Your Heart

1. When do you find it most difficult to be patient? When is it most difficult to be understanding?

2. How can you put yourself in someone else's shoes to help yourself grow in patience and understanding?

3. Reread Luke 2:41–52. How would you have responded in that situation? How is that similar to the way Mary responded? How is it different?

Fiat

Think about the relationship in your life that brings you to a boil the quickest. It could be a relationship with a neighbor, a friend, a coworker, your spouse, or even your teacher or boss. Ask God to give you the grace of patient understanding for that person. The next time you feel yourself nearing your breaking point, lift those spiritual weights by turning your thoughts away from your rising emotions and seek instead to understand the other person better in that moment.

Prayer

God, give me a heart that seeks unity, a heart that seeks to understand others. When I feel frustration rising inside me, give me the grace to choose patience. When I feel annoyed, let me embrace that thorn in my side and trust that through it, you are strengthening my spirit. When my soul squirms and burns within me in the grind of virtuous living, help me continue to hold and lift those spiritual weights. Mary, pray for me, that like you, I may put love before anger and become a model of patient understanding. Amen.

DETERMINED COOPERATION WITH GOD

Wedding in Cana

On the third day there was a wedding in Cana of Galilee, and the mother of Jesus was there. Jesus and his disciples had also been invited to the wedding. When the wine gave out, the mother of Jesus said to him, "They have no wine." And Jesus said to her, "Woman, what concern is that to you and to me? My hour has not yet come." His mother said to the servants, "Do whatever he tells you."

—John 2:1–5

Like many newlyweds, when my husband and I went on our honeymoon, we were flat broke. So, while we were at the all-inclusive resort—a trip given to us by a family member—we took great advantage of all its free perks. It isn't any wonder that, both being avid jocks, we wanted to take a kayak out into the open ocean and snorkel there.

We rowed until we were far from shore, and then decided that if we both leaned over opposite sides of the boat at the exact same time, we could put our faces in the water and see the fish without flipping the kayak.

The plan was flawless.

But lo and behold, I leaned too far over the edge before my husband had even slipped his snorkel on. In a splash, the whole thing capsized and we were tossed into the ocean.

Huffing and puffing, we righted the boat, setting it back atop the tranquil water.

Phew, I thought. *Everything's fine. Thank goodness.*

Then I looked at my husband's snorkel-less face and my heart plummeted.

"The snorkel's gone!" I shouted.

My husband's eyes widened with panic, his thoughts meshing with mine immediately: We'd have to pay for the missing equipment, and that would cost a pretty penny.

Heck, we didn't even have an ugly penny.

"We have to find it," I said resolutely.

So began our new plan.

We'd comb the ocean together—one of us swimming beside the kayak searching the ocean floor while the other paddled the kayak and kept a lookout for sharks.

Never mind that the ocean stretches far and wide. Never mind that the current could have pulled it any-where. Never mind that the chances of finding the dang thing were slim to ain't-ever-gonna-happen. And definitely never mind that the snorkel was freaking *blue*.

Armed with the naiveté and determination of newlyweds, we began our search.

We swam back and forth all day long. After hours of searching, the sun was beginning to set.

"That's it," my husband said, throwing his hands into the air in frustration. "We should go back and tell them we lost it."

"No," I said. Deep in my heart, I knew—I *knew*—we could find this thing. I didn't know how. I didn't know when. But there was a strange surety in my bones. "We can do this. Let's try a little longer."

He set his jaw with determination, squinting against the setting sun. Then he put his finger in the air, testing the breeze. My husband's fierce blue eyes darted back toward a jetty of rocks, and his face lit with revelation. "The wind is blowing northwest," he said, then looked to me like I should understand. I shrugged as best as I could while treading water.

He pointed toward the jetty. "We capsized there and the wind is blowing northwest. Which means, if we limit our search to right *there*"—he gestured in a direction I assumed was northwest—"we should find it."

I nodded, fueled once again by the hope of having a plan. One that didn't involve perfect balance or a run-in with sharks.

With my strong, smart husband paddling the kayak by my side, we swam from one side of the perimeter to the other. Then back again. Down. Back. Until something odd glimmered from the ocean floor. I squinted to get a better look.

The snorkel!

I screamed and popped up out of the water.

We had found our lost blue snorkel in the middle of the big blue ocean.

All this got me thinking about a wedding. Not ours, surprisingly. But one that happened thousands of years ago in Cana of Galilee.

Mary and Jesus were both there, enjoying all the things people normally enjoy about a great wedding. The music. The dancing. The wine. Being there to support the newlyweds, who I'm guessing, like many newlyweds, were flat broke. It wouldn't be surprising if Mary, being the holy, selfless woman she is, offered to help with the serving.

Huffing and puffing, I imagine her clearing plates and mopping up spilled drinks, until the night grew late.

Phew, she may have thought, wiping her brow. *Everything's going fine. Thank goodness.*

But lo and behold, at some point, the wedding hit a snafu, as so many weddings do.

And when she peeked into the wineless cisterns, her heart plummeted. Knowing her, she probably looked everywhere for an extra stock of wine. After a lot of searching, there'd been no sign of it.

Her eyes must've widened with panic, her thoughts darting to one conclusion: The hosts would have to get more wine, and for a group of this size, that would cost a pretty penny.

A pretty penny the new couple did not have.

So she ran to Jesus, the One she could trust to come up with a brilliant plan.

She might have found him among the wedding guests and pulled him aside privately, wringing her hands on her apron. "They have no wine!" she said.

"Woman, what concern is that to you and to me? My hour has not yet come."

His hour.

The hour of ministry. The hour of his great sacrifice. The hour of his Body and Blood, which is, consequently, the hour of our salvation.

Perhaps she watched her Son's fierce, dark eyes dart back toward the empty cisterns. Despite his apparent refusal, he was coming up with a plan.

At his side, Mary may have nodded, fueled by the hope of God's plan, armed with determination and a burning desire to do whatever Jesus said. She trusted him more than anything and was willing to do whatever it took to fix this problem.

Never mind that the nearest vendor would be closed at this time of night. Never mind that even if they *did* get the drinks, they'd have to lug the heavy jars all the way back before any of the guests realized the wine had run out. And definitely never mind that the chances of that happening were slim to ain't-ever-gonna-happen.

Deep in her heart, she knew—she *knew*—Jesus could fix this. She may not have known how. She may not have known how long it would take. But there was a strange surety in her bones.

So she turned to the others. "Do whatever he tells you."

⚜ A Soul That Magnifies ⚜

Determined Cooperation With God

Like me treading water in the middle of the ocean, Mary probably had no idea what Jesus' plan would entail or how it would play out, but she trusted her Son. She knew he would take care of it somehow. That was the important thing. It wasn't how much Mary understood. What matters is what she did, despite her understanding. The thing to note is how she was *responding* to Jesus. And how did she respond to Jesus? The same way she responded to him her whole life: She trusted him and told everyone else to trust him, too. She surrendered to God's will and then, with a steel resolve, got down to business working with him to make it happen.

Because let's be real. Our plans are often weak and short-sighted. (What would my husband and I have done if we *actually* ran into a shark? I have no idea.) God's plans, however, are much fuller, much richer. Much more comprehensive and well thought out. When we listen to and cooperate with *his* plans, things tend to work out much better.

For example, Mary may have been focused on getting wine for that evening, which was great. But Jesus?

He not only prepared wine for that evening, but also prepared us for the wine for eternity.

Mary may have been thinking of saving the reputation of the newlyweds, which was wonderful. Jesus, on the other hand, thought of saving their reputations *and* saving the souls of his very own Bride.

For just as Jesus saved the wedding hosts by changing water into wine, so he also saved us by changing wine into his Blood at the Last Supper and by offering the water and blood that gushed forth from his body on Calvary.

And who besides God could have dreamed up a plan like that?

Ponder in Your Heart

1. Oftentimes—at least in my own experience—God's plans don't make much sense on paper, but when I follow his direction anyway, everything miraculously (and beautifully) works out. What is Jesus calling you to do today? How can you trust him and determinedly cooperate with him to fulfill that call?

2. Do you have any "lost snorkel" (or problem) in your life that needs to be addressed? How can you work together with God to fix it?

3. Reread John 2:1–11. How does Mary's determined cooperation shine through in this passage?

Fiat

Pray, listen, and do whatever he tells you.

Prayer

Mary, standing beside you that night, Jesus miraculously filled the cups of all who were at the wedding so that they could all take of it and drink. He echoed that sentiment at the Last Supper. Now, thousands of years later, our priests hold up the chalice in Jesus' place, as Jesus once again miraculously fills the cup so that we may all take of it and drink. All this happens for us now because you said yes so long ago. You walked beside him with determined cooperation to redeem the world as with one heart. Help me to also enter into that mysterious adventure. Help me to walk beside Jesus with unwavering determination, so that through my life—through my yes—God will do amazing, miraculous things. Amen.

LOYALTY

Who Is My Mother?

While he was still speaking to the crowds, his mother and his brothers were standing outside, wanting to speak to him. Someone told him, "Look, your mother and your brothers are standing outside, wanting to speak to you." But to the one who had told him this, Jesus replied, "Who is my mother, and who are my brothers?" And pointing to his disciples, he said, "Here are my mother and my brothers! For whoever does the will of my Father in heaven is my brother and sister and mother."

—Matthew 12:46–50

I've learned that when God asks me to do something, I should do it, even if—and especially *when*—it makes zero sense on paper.

So when God nudged me to write my first book, I cocked my head in confusion, and then cracked open my laptop for the first time in years. I typed and typed, spilling my heart onto those pages until, finally, I wrote the very last word.

"Now what?" I asked God.

As it turned out, God's next harebrained idea was to get it published.

"You want me to *what*?" It didn't make any sense, but for whatever reason, God was asking me to do it. So I did. I researched publishers who might be interested in a Catholic devotional for moms, collecting them in an excel sheet. I was only familiar with two of them. Two biggies.

I sent my book to Big Name Dream Publisher #1 and leaned back in my chair, clasping my hands behind my head. I knew I wouldn't hear anything back. All I had to do was wait a few months and move on.

I heard back in one week.

They loved it. They wanted more.

My jaw dropped as I read their email. *Holy heck, God! Are you going to get this published with Big Name Dream Publisher #1 on the first shot?*

Giddy, I sent them the full manuscript—my whole heart in written word. Then I waited and waited, my heart churning inside my chest.

Finally—FINALLY—I heard back.

I raced to my computer and flung open the email.

Rejection.

Pain stabbed my soul, but God nudged me to keep going.

Wounded, I crossed off Big Name Dream Publisher #1 in a bright red stripe on my excel sheet and moved on to Big Name Dream Publisher #2.

Soon, another red stripe splashed across Excel.

Publisher #3. Another red stripe.

That was it. Three strikes and I was out. It seemed like the end of the road. There were plenty more publishers on the list, but my heart couldn't take anymore. It hurt too much.

I closed the excel sheet and resolved to never look at it again. Had I misheard God's call to write that book in the first place?

I didn't care. I left it behind and lived blissfully with no publishers. No rejection. No worries. There was a peace in that, like God was giving me permission to let it all go.

Then, out of nowhere at the end of July, Jesus tugged at my heart again. He gently pulled me back to my excel sheet.

"What am I doing here?" I hissed at God, staring at the words onscreen. Was he trying to remind me of my failure? Was this some sort of sick, twisted lesson in humility?

Amid the long list of publishers, my eyes landed on one innocently tucked in the middle of the list. It was almost as if it were beckoning me.

I had never heard of it. Some group of religious sisters. A publisher called Pauline Books & Media.

"Cast your nets one more time," Jesus said. "Right there."

I rolled my eyes. Hadn't we been through this? I knew how it was going to end. But what was one more red stripe? I sighed and submitted a small sample of my work, awaiting the all-too-familiar sting of rejection.

Days went by. Then weeks.

Then I actually heard back. They loved it. They wanted more.

Oh, no, I thought. *Not again*.

But I'd come too far to turn back. Sweating, I uploaded my full manuscript—my whole heart in written form—and clicked Send.

Not long later, I got an email from one of the sisters. She was the acquisitions editor. And, as it turned out, she had received her title of both Sister and acquisitions editor at the end of July.

The end of July? I wondered.

Wasn't that the *exact* time Jesus pulled me toward my crimson-stained excel sheet?

God hit me with the hard truth that he'd been waiting for this sister to step onto the scene and become the champion of my book.

Finally, *finally*, I started seeing God's hand orchestrating everything. I hadn't misheard the call after all. God had been leading me the whole time. And this path Jesus led me down? It has grown me not only in my writing, but also in my relationship with him. Not to mention, it plugged me into a totally new-to-me community. A family, of sorts. In short, it's been better than I ever could have dreamed. The journey didn't look the way I planned. The path was paved with rejection. But, in reality, those rejections were a gentle redirection, a loving invitation into a deeper relationship with Jesus.

Mary must've understood this to some degree, and when she went to see her Son during his ministry, her eyes may have landed on the One who was innocently tucked in the middle of the crowd, beckoning her.

Surely, she was giddy with excitement. There he was—right there! Her Son. Her Savior. Her whole heart. What she wouldn't do to get one moment alone with him. To hug him, perhaps, or kiss the beard on his cheek. To tell him how proud she was or how much she loved him.

"Excuse me," she may have whispered to one of his apostles, never wanting to distract others from her Son. "Could I speak with Jesus?"

Knowing who Mary was, I imagine he nodded and sneaked through the crowd to retrieve her answer.

So she waited, totally unperturbed, knowing Jesus was going to do . . . *something*. Whatever it was, he would do it in his way, in his time.

Moments passed. Then minutes.

Finally, *finally*, she heard his voice. Her Son.

"Who is my Mother?" he boomed across the crowd, as he pointed at the people gathered there. "Here are my mother and my brothers! For whoever does the will of my Father in heaven is my brother and sister and mother."

Perhaps her heart ached at his words. The seeming rejection made it feel like this was the end of the road. Maybe she wouldn't get that time alone with him after all. She could have given up. Could have gone home.

But she had come too far. There was no going back now.

Fierce loyalty to her Son propelled her to be by his side—even from a distance, even in a crowd. Perhaps she looked around at all the unfamiliar faces and recognized that Jesus' words were not a rejection, but a loving invitation into a deeper relationship with him and with each other.

It was his plan all along.

To bring us all together. You. Me. His Mother. All of us. In that moment, Jesus was inviting all of us to be part of God's family.

So Mary didn't brood over her seeming rejection. No, because of Mary's loyalty to her Son and his mission, she willingly threw out her own plan and swapped it for his. She tossed aside that one moment she'd wished to call on her Son so she could spend the rest of eternity calling you daughter.

❧ A Soul That Magnifies ❧

Loyalty

In this day and age, almost everyone has followers. We can walk around with a huge following tucked in the safety of our back pocket. People "like" our messages by giving them a blue thumbs up or a bright red heart. If people don't like what we've shared, they can ignore it or make a negative comment. Perhaps because of that, love has become misconstrued to mean agreement. If you agree with people, you love them. On the flip side, if you disagree with people, you hate them.

But that's not the case. Mary and Jesus show that here.

Jesus seems to have disagreed with Mary about this particular moment in his ministry. She wanted to be together with him one-on-one. He wanted to include everyone. Instead of getting huffy and offended, however, Mary chose to stick by Jesus' side. To love him. To be there with him and for him, no matter what. Mary's loyalty to her Son propelled her to be by his side in the first place. Then, even when things didn't go her way, loyalty propelled her to *stay* by his side.

Loving people we agree with is easy. Anyone can do that. Even tax collectors can, as Jesus points out (see

Matthew 5:46). But we can offer a greater, deeper love when we disagree with someone and still choose to want their good anyway.

Loyalty, then—that faithful devotion to someone else—is something altogether different from the "following" we do on social media. It means being there with others and for others—wanting their good—through the ups and downs of life. Loyalty doesn't cut people out based on a disagreement. It's an unwavering, unfailing, ever-present love.

That's the type of love we're called to give God and others. Not the easy, shallow, temporary stuff, but the real, deep, nitty-gritty, unconditional kind of love that comes through loyalty to another.

Ponder in Your Heart

1. Whom or what are you loyal to? How do you show it?

2. How can you be loyal to God and what he calls you to do, even when it makes zero sense on paper?

3. How do you usually respond to rejection? Have you ever experienced a time when God turned a seeming rejection into an invitation to a deeper relationship with him?

4. Reread Matthew 12:46–50. How does Mary's loyalty shine through in this passage?

Fiat

Follow Jesus by loving everyone like family, even when you disagree with each other.

Prayer

Mary, thank you for being such a beautiful example of loyalty to Jesus. No matter where he led, you willingly followed, trusting that he knew what he was doing. Even when his words seemed confusing. Even when the path was paved with sorrow. Even when it seemed like Jesus had gone totally mad. You knew his voice and you followed it. You understood that everything he does is intentional. Everything he does has meaning. Every single thing he does is always about love, always about friendship with God, always about salvation. Pray for me, Mother, that I may also be willing to unite with him in that mission, even if it means I must swap my plans for his and trust him as he leads me through this life. Jesus, fill my heart with loyalty to you and your mission, so that through me, you may make your Kingdom come. Amen.

COMPASSION

The Crucifixion

When Jesus saw his mother and the disciple whom he loved standing beside her, he said to his mother, "Woman, here is your son." Then he said to the disciple, "Here is your mother." And from that hour the disciple took her into his own home.

—John 19:26–27

Crash! BOOM!

Even from a different room, I knew whatever had just happened was bad.

Then came the cry of pain.

My son.

I ran toward the sound, my heart hiccupping into my throat.

I sprinted through one room, then rounded the corner of another, ready to race in and assess the damage. Ready to cuddle and kiss. Ready to . . . I don't know, do whatever a mother is supposed to do in situations like this.

But my husband had gotten there first and was cradling our son in his lap, absorbing the little boy's wild howls of pain.

Good, I thought, shrinking back out of sight. *My husband is much better than I am at making people feel better.*

But there's something about pain that pulls a woman's heart toward it. So, I merely stood there, on the other side of the wall, as my heart ached inside my chest, reaching for my son, longing to console him.

It hurt to hear him and not wrap my arms around him. To do nothing to help. To be absent when he was in pain. I wished I could rush in and take the boy from his father's hands, to alleviate his ache and my own.

But my son was better off with his dad—the guy who is way more compassionate and tender than I am. The man with a gift for knowing what to do to make people feel better. The father who can turn tears into laughter at the drop of a hat.

I, on the other hand, flounder about, wondering what to do besides coddle and kiss and rock back and forth. When people are in pain in my lap, their cries continue for long stretches of time.

And then it happened.

Despite being in the capable hands and heart of his father, my son called my name. I peeked around the doorframe.

"MOOOOOMMMYY!!!!" my son cried, choked by tears, blood already pooling on his lip.

My husband rose from the floor, carrying him to me.

"Here she is," my husband cooed gently. "Here's Mommy."

The little boy reached for me, clinging to my body with all his might.

I kissed his head and shushed his aching sniffles. I sang and rocked him gently. Whispered over and over into his ear that he was okay.

Finally, I could get a look at the injury and wrap my arms around his pain. Could squeeze the hurt away with a hug, suffocating it with love. Could finally, *finally*, extinguish these burning flames in our hearts.

I looked into his eyes, those eyes so full of anguish. I would have done anything for him in that moment.

"Would you like to read a book with me?" I asked.

"No."

"Would you like to play ball?"

"No."

"Would you like a snack?"

He shook his head.

"Would you like more hugs from Mom?"

He nodded, his lip puckering as he fell back into my chest.

So I let him stay there on my lap, getting cuddled and hugged back to life.

As I sat there, rocking this boy—my sweet, sweet son—I couldn't help but think of Mary and how her bleeding heart must have also been made of supernatural steel.

I mean, I could hardly bear to hear my son's cries after he sprained his thumb. How much more would Mary's heart have been strangled at the sight of Jesus' crucifixion?

How could she possibly bear it?

The jeers. The shouts. The ugly words. The sound of metal through flesh and wood.

Even from the middle of the crowd, Mary could probably tell that what was happening was bad.

Then came his cries of pain.

Her Son.

I imagine she ran toward the sound, her heart hiccupping into her throat.

Perhaps she squeezed between a couple of people, then rushed through others until she was at the foot of the cross, ready to race in and assess the damage. Ready to cuddle and kiss. Ready to . . . do whatever a mother is supposed to do in a horrific situation like that.

Maybe her shuffling feet jolted to a stop as she watched the soldiers hammering long spikes into Jesus' wrists and feet.

What can I do? she may have thought, fighting the urge to reach out and touch him for fear of adding to his injury.

But there's something about pain that pulls a woman's heart toward it. So, she stood, planted in place at the foot of the cross as they lifted him high. Surely her heart ached as she reached for her Son, longing to console him.

I can't imagine how much it must have hurt to not wrap her arms around him. To do nothing to help. To be unable to reach out and touch him when he was in pain.

And then it happened.

Despite being in the capable hands and heart of his Father, Jesus called out for his Mother.

"Woman," Jesus called from above her, his blood pouring down the wooden pole.

I wonder if she looked up into his eyes and found them full of anguish. I bet she would have done anything for him in that moment.

Would he like some wine perhaps, to dull the pain? Or a cloth to sop up the blood and cover his most private areas? Would he want her to reach up and caress his bloody foot? Or would he ask for desperate prayers to his Abba he kept calling out to?

But Jesus only had one request. "Behold your son."

He no longer wished for Mary to comfort *him*, but her new child. The child Jesus gave to her in that moment. His most beloved friend.

You.

Me.

All of us.

So, today, as we carry our crosses through life, Mary rushes to our side. Perhaps her heart still squeezes inside her chest as she hears the cries of her children. I wonder if she looks into our eyes and finds them full of anguish sometimes. And, in those moments, I bet she would do anything for us—anything at all—so long as it brings us closer to Christ.

❧ A Soul That Magnifies ❧

Compassion

Though it surely splintered her Immaculate Heart into millions of tiny pieces to watch her Son—the One she loved more than life itself—be whipped, condemned, abandoned, spat upon, spiked to a tree, and lifted up for all to revile and jeer at him, Mary *had* to be there. If compassion hadn't moved her to Christ's side, her heart would have no doubt engulfed itself in the flame of agony.

Being the good Mother she is, she had to try to console, to wrap her arms around her Son's pain and suffocate it with love. But she couldn't.

Surely, *that* was her greatest grievance.

It was only after Jesus died—after death had greedily absorbed every last ounce of his pain—that Mary was allowed to cradle him in her arms. Even then, when he was dead and bloody, she probably held and rocked him. She had to. Her mother's heart would've demanded it of her. Though he was completely lifeless, she'd still have the urge to console and nurture her Son.

Compassion compelled Mary throughout her entire life. It propelled her to Elizabeth's side after the Annunciation. It moved her to help the newlyweds at the wedding in Cana. Finally, it pulled her to the foot of the cross.

And now, through Jesus' command that she behold us, her intense desire to alleviate pain transfers to us. We are her children. Jesus asked her to behold and console *us*, and she never disobeys him.

We emulate Mary's example every time we choose to be compassionate with those around us. Friends. Neighbors. Coworkers. Spouses. Nieces and nephews. Strangers, even. When we mourn with those who mourn. When we reach out to those who are sick, lonely, or hurt. When we hoist someone else's cross upon our shoulders and carry it with them. Any time we tenderly care for those who are suffering, we console the Sacred Heart of Jesus and share compassion with others.

Ponder in Your Heart

1. How can you console the Sacred Heart of Jesus today?

2. On the Cross, Jesus gave Mary to each of us to be our Mother. How does a child show love for her mother? How can you show Mary your love for her?

3. How can you show compassion toward the people God places in your life?

4. Reread John 19:25–27 and imagine what that moment must have been like for a grief-stricken

mother whose intense love for Jesus now covers you. How can you allow yourself to be held by Mary today?

Fiat

Behold others and *be held* by your Mother.

Prayer

Abba, I cry out to you, craving to be held in your loving and capable hands. Because you are such a good Father, I know you will never forsake or abandon me. Jesus, even in the moment of your greatest anguish, you thought not of yourself but others. Though you felt abandoned, you did not abandon me. Even in the darkest hour, you brought forth light. Thank you for the Mother you so compassionately gave to me that day. Mary, Mother of Jesus, please be a mother to me now. Rush to my side as I falter beneath the weight of my cross. Alleviate my pain and assuage my suffering. Take my hand in yours and walk with me, step-by-step, all the way to heaven. O sweet Mother Mary, comforter of the afflicted, whisper over and over in my ear that I will be okay because I belong to your Son. Mary, sweet Mother, pray for me that I may have a tender heart toward others. Open my eyes to the suffering of those around me and help me show compassion in my interactions with those whom God places in my path. Amen.

PRAYERFULNESS

Devoted Themselves with One Accord to Prayer

When they had entered the city, they went to the room upstairs where they were staying, Peter, and John, and James, and Andrew, Philip and Thomas, Bartholomew and Matthew, James son of Alphaeus, and Simon the Zealot, and Judas son of James. All these were constantly devoting themselves to prayer, together with certain women, including Mary the mother of Jesus, as well as his brothers.

—Acts 1:13–14

I try to pray a Rosary every day. *Try* being the key word.

Some days I pray the Rosary, ticking off Hail Marys on my fingers as I nurse and rock my infant back to sleep. Some days my toddler creeps down the steps, lured by the lamp light in my office, wanting to slip onto my lap before anyone else. Some days no one comes down at all—it's just me and my rosary. Those days are the worst. On those days, I still can't get my life together enough to focus on the holy mysteries and I have no one to blame but myself.

But the one thing that never changes is that every morning I rise long before the sun, armed with caffeine, some blessed beads, and the unwavering hope that today will be the day I finally do it right.

"How was your Rosary today?" my husband asked one day as the sun arced high across the sky.

I shrugged. That day, I had flown through the entire thing on autopilot, cranking out all the prayers without thinking. I was actually confused when I boogied forward to the next bead and discovered it was the very last one. How was I already on the last bead? What mystery was I even on, anyway? I had to squint into the depths of my memory to figure it out and press forward, asking for the fruit of that mystery one more time.

"I couldn't stay focused," I confessed.

"That's okay," my husband reassured me. "It's okay to waste time with Jesus."

I did a double take. Waste time? I pondered the phrase and shook my head. "I didn't waste time."

"What do you mean?" He cocked a brow. Had his Type-A, perfectionistic wife really said that spacing out for twenty minutes *wasn't* a waste of time?

"I asked Mary to pray for me over fifty times," I said in awe, suddenly understanding the power of the

Rosary. The strength of that revelation could have blown my hair backward.

Mary spent her whole *life* praying. Talking to Jesus. If Mary ever rubbed her swollen, pregnant belly and cooed at him in her womb, that was prayer. When Jesus first woke up in the morning, and she talked to him, that was prayer. At breakfast, when they played, when she taught him things, or bathed him? Prayer, prayer, prayer, prayer. Even when she tucked him in at the end of the day. That, too, was prayer.

Even after Jesus died and was buried in a stranger's tomb, she undoubtedly sat, stunned, locked in the upper room. I imagine, after a full lifetime of doing nothing but praying, she didn't know what *else* to do. So probably even then she prayed. And, after Jesus beat death, came back to life, and ascended into Heaven, what did she do? She devoted herself to prayer. Because that Lady doesn't do anything half-heartedly. Especially pray.

"*I* might not have been focused," I said to my husband, "but Mary never prays half-heartedly. Kind of like being in a group project where one person does all the work."

My husband grimaced, knowing I don't like people to do anything for me. Let alone do *everything* for me. "How do you feel about that?"

I smirked. "I'll let you know when I get my final grade."

"Well, you don't have much to worry about. I think that person in your group knows exactly what the Teacher wants."

I smiled, my heart warmed at the thought of Mary's closeness with her Son. She knows the Teacher—our Rabboni—better than anyone else, and she's willing to share that gift with me if I let her. She *wants* to do the work. She wants to bring us to her Son. Immense gratitude swelled inside me at the thought.

All I had to do was show up and let Mary lead me by the hand.

"I bet the Teacher would appreciate a little effort on my part, too," I admitted, feeling the bumpy beads of my rosary in my back pocket. I might not be perfect. I might not always be focused. But I would choose to show up. Not necessarily because my final grade depended on it, but because I really, really love my Teacher and the Lady leading my group.

So the next morning, I rose long before the sun, armed with caffeine and some blessed beads, as I devoted myself to prayer with the understanding that, no matter what, the next twenty minutes wouldn't be a waste.

❧ A Soul That Magnifies ❧

Prayerfulness

Prayer can be tough to explain to a little kid, especially when they can't *see* God or fully understand who he is. So, when I describe it to my kids, I simply say that prayer is talking to Jesus.

And, by that definition, Mary's whole life must've been filled with prayer. Can you imagine a mother *not* talking to her child?

Heck, pretty much all I do is talk to my kids. All day, every day.

I imagine Mary was the same way. Except, when she talked to her Son, it was prayer because he *is* God.

She didn't always have to pray with her hands clasped together, her gaze raised to the heavens, the way we see her in statues. Prayer, to her, was simply a way of life. When she was overjoyed? She turned to God (see Luke 1:46–55). Worried? She ran to Jesus (see John 2:1–5). Distraught? She clung to Jesus then, too (see John 19:25). And then, after watching Jesus ascend into heaven, what did she do? She devoted herself to prayer, yet again (see Acts 1:13–14). No matter how she felt or what she was doing, Mary kept God company. Even now, as Queen of Heaven and Earth, she spends her time talking to Jesus and praying for us. Mary, then, is the ever-present model of how we are to pray—constantly, intimately, and out of deep love for Jesus.

Ponder in Your Heart

1. What does prayer mean to you? What does prayer time normally look like for you?

2. What would it look like to devote yourself to prayer more fully?

3. Reread Acts 1:13–14. What can you learn about the way Mary prays? How can you pray more like her? How can you trust in her intercession?

Fiat

You're not talking to yourself when you pray, though it may feel like it sometimes. Keep in mind that Jesus is listening and responding. When you pray, think of him and talk *to* him.

Prayer

Lord Jesus, you are our good Teacher. You are our Rabboni. Thank you for the gift of prayer, and for going so far as to teach us how to pray well. How is it that the Creator of the galaxies wants to hear from me? What on earth could I possibly say to the One who holds the whole world in his hand? Give me a heart that longs to love you, a heart that yearns to talk to you. Holy Spirit, prompt me to pray and give me the self-discipline to respond to those urgings. Give me the boldness to show up to prayer, to stand before you and speak. Help me be a woman who devotes herself to prayer. Sweet Mother Mary, on the days my prayer time is interrupted or cut short, pray for me. On the days I can't seem to focus, pray for me. On the days I question the power of prayer, pray for me. On the days I fail to show up, pray for me. Holy Mary, Mother of God, pray for me, now and at the hour of my death. Amen.

ZEAL

Sharing Jesus' Story

When the day of Pentecost had come, they were all together in one place.

—Acts 2:1

"Mom, will you read me a book?"

The question was so innocent coming from the lips of my five-year-old son.

I sat on the couch, nursing my infant. Reading was one of my favorite things in the world, but there was so much else to do. Nurse the baby. Burp the baby. Clean the house. Cook dinner.

I sighed.

If only I had more hands.

I adjusted the baby in my lap, and then glanced up at my son, whose big brown eyes pleaded for attention. For love. I pushed everything else out of mind. "Sure, kiddo. Which one?"

He whipped out a book from behind his back, one he'd been hiding in hopes I would say yes to his request. "This one!"

His own picture stared back at me from the hardcover, and I cocked my head to read the title, though I didn't need to. *Welcome to the World, Baby Boy*.

My son's baby book.

"Ah, this one," I said, patting the couch, inviting him to sit next to me. "This is one of my favorite books of all time."

He happily plopped down and leaned against me to scour his own life's story. He'd heard the stories a gazillion times, of course, but didn't remember—couldn't possibly remember—what it was like to be there in those stories from his past. No, that responsibility rested on my shoulders. I was the keeper of his long-lost memories. The guardian of moments otherwise swallowed by history. Somewhere deep down, he understood this, so he pointed out the pictures and peppered me with questions.

Will you tell me the story of when I was born?

Where were we in this picture with all the snow? Was that when you and Dad took us skiing in Colorado?

Will you tell me about my Baptism again? How my first word was "hi" and when you held me at the front of church, I said "hi" over and over to everyone in the pews?

I recounted each detail, the moments singed in my memory by love and repetitive storytelling. Even now, I could practically hear my son's whimper—not scream—when the doctor pulled him from my womb in an emergency c-section. Could feel the frigid, refreshing wind of the Rocky Mountains in February. Could smell the chrism oil they drenched him with at his Baptism. The memories were so real, so vivid, it was as if I was reliving them each time I told the tale.

At the end of the last story, my son closed the book. He looked up at me, smiling. "Can we read it again?"

In that moment, it hit me. All those stories about the Annunciation? The Visitation? The Nativity, the Presentation, and perhaps even the Finding of Jesus in the Temple? They must have been stories that Mary told. After all, Jesus was either unborn or an infant in most of them, and by the time the apostles came around, Joseph had already died. Only one member of the Holy Family remained as a credible source to tell those stories.

Mary.

I imagine the apostles thirsted for backstory and history on this Jesus guy, the one they'd come to know was the Messiah. And who better to recount those days leading up to Jesus' birth and infancy than Jesus' own Mother?

Perhaps the apostles plopped down beside her in the days before Pentecost as they were waiting in the upper room, desperate to scour the Messiah's own life story. With Joseph gone, Mary would have been the sole keeper of those memories. The guardian of moments otherwise swallowed by history. Somewhere deep down, the apostles probably understood this. Perhaps they even pointed that out, peppering her with questions and begging to hear stories about Jesus.

"Sure," she may have said, eager to tell stories about her beloved Son. "Which one?"

Will you tell us the story of his birth?

Will you tell us about his Presentation?

You had to flee to Egypt after that? Why? Tell us the story.

"Ah, that one," she may have said after each request, inviting them to come close. "That is one of my favorite stories of all time."

Surely, she could recount each detail, the moments singed in her memory by love and repetitive storytelling. Perhaps she could nearly hear her Son's voice the first moment it entered the world. Could feel the frigid, refreshing wind of the Judean Mountains as they crossed from Nazareth to Bethlehem. Could smell the incense in the Temple when Jesus was consecrated to God. The memories were so real, so vivid, it may have been as though she was reliving them each time she told the tale. No doubt the apostles took her words to heart. For when the Holy Spirit descended upon them at Pentecost and filled them with zeal, they too shared those stories so the whole world would come to know Jesus.

Now, thanks to Mary's passionate dedication to telling people about Jesus—and the apostles' zeal in spreading those stories far and wide—we can relive those moments, too. And, at the end of the last story, one question rises to my lips.

Can I read it again?

⚜ A Soul That Magnifies ⚜

Zeal

I find myself loving those stories (and Mary!) even more now. Because of her zeal—her passionate desire and enthusiasm to share Jesus and the Gospel with others—those stories from Jesus' early years have been preserved through the ages.

Mary, then, plays a pivotal role not only in physically bearing the Word, but also in witnessing to it through her words and actions. She not only *bore* the Incarnate Word, but then in a sense, she *spoke* the word—Scripture itself—for others to hear, so that all of her children (including us!) could know the story of salvation.

Like Mary, we are also called to share Jesus with others. And, also like Mary, God calls us to do that in our own unique way. Be it through written word, a one-on-one conversation, or posting about Jesus on social media. It could be as simple as sharing a story about what God has done in our own lives. We can even evangelize without any words at all, simply by living as a clear reflection of God's love for others.

Ponder in Your Heart

1. Do you live zealously for God? How can you use your unique gifts and personality to show zeal for God?

2. Is there anyone in your life who might be uplifted by a story about Jesus? How can you share the Word with them?

3. Reread Luke 1–2 as though they were family stories being told by a loving mother. What's it like to get a peek inside Jesus' baby book?

Fiat

Talk about Jesus with someone in your life.

Prayer

God, your story is the greatest love story of all time. How is it possible that I am the object of your fierce love? I am the one you pursue—the one you have pursued since the beginning of time. Open my mind to understand that reality and fill my heart with such great love of you that I can't help but share your story with others. Mary, our beautiful Theotokos, *bearer of God, thank you for giving Jesus to us in flesh and word. Pray for us, O Holy Mother of God, that we too may have the enthusiasm and passion to share Christ with others, in word and deed. Amen.*

EPILOGUE

Thy Kingdom Come

My two-year-old daughter is obsessed with gorillas. Not the real ones, necessarily, but the stationary ones she can ride on the carousel at our zoo. There, a plethora of animals spin around and around like some sort of dizzy, plastic stampede. There's an ostrich. A hummingbird. Horses, of course. Even a triceratops.

But, no. My daughter always, always picks the gorilla.

I don't know what it is about the gorilla that captured her attention. Maybe it's his painted black fur. Or the way he crouches down waiting for a passenger. Maybe it just so happened to be my daughter's first-choice-turned-forever-love.

Whatever the case, when we crossed through the entrance of the zoo one day, my daughter only had one thing on her mind. "Ride animals!" she shouted and then pounded her chest with her tiny fists. "'Rilla say 'ooh ooh'!"

"There are *real* gorillas here," I said. "Would you like to go see them?"

My daughter's eyes widened and a smile exploded across her face. "YES!!!! 'Rilla say, 'ooh ooh'!" She pounded her chest again.

"We can go see them in their houses," I said, chuckling, "but I don't know if they'll hit their chest like that." I'd been taking my kids to the zoo for nearly a decade and the most exciting thing the gorillas had done was munch on lettuce and nap against the window.

The little girl was unfazed. She could see *real* gorillas? That was a dream come true.

So, just like that, we were off to the jungles of Africa, looking for giant apes hidden among the trees. Only, in this jungle, there were very well-paved paths leading to an observatory with air-conditioning and walls made of impenetrable glass. My kind of jungle.

I swung open the door of the observatory and ushered my daughter inside, and then we headed to the wall of windows. There, dwarfed by the ginormous glass, was a sheet of paper. A warning. Apparently, the male gorillas had been in a fight, and that was why they were bleeding. My two-year-old, however, clearly couldn't read that poster. Blinded by excitement, she danced in front of the windows and stared out at the big, strong gorillas. They looked just like the one on the carousel. Except these gorillas moved and snorted and snarled and bled.

"'Rilla say, 'ooh ooh!'" my daughter chirped beside me, holding the rail in front of the window.

"I don't know if they'll say that here," I reminded her, rubbing her floppy blond hair.

Then, from the shadows of the exhibit, a huge gorilla lumbered forward. He stomped to the top of the hill directly in front of the observatory—directly in front of *us*—until he was standing in full view, his horrific scowl all too visible. He stared us down with a fierce, unbridled fury burning in his eyes. My daughter slipped her little hand in mine and squeezed tight, unable to take her eyes off of her beloved gorilla despite the trembling in her fingers.

Then, as if on cue, the animal rose onto his hind legs, roared with bared teeth, and pounded his chest with thick, angry fists.

My daughter desperately grasped for me, and I scooped her up, holding her close as she buried her face in my neck. The poor girl was shaking. Heck, *I* was shaking.

"Can we *not* go see 'rillas?" she whispered. "That big 'rilla scary."

I wrapped my arms around her and hugged, not caring that she was squeezing my neck a little too tight.

In that moment, I understood. Out of all the evidence that points to the existence of God—and to the reality that we are made in his image and likeness—I find the most convicting of all to be the practice of virtue.

You see, we, too, are animals in the animal kingdom. We, too, have the urge to be the alpha. On our own, it's easy to slip back into our animalistic tendencies. To stride pridefully to the top of the hill, beat our chest, and scare others away in an attempt to best them.

Because that's how the animal world works.

The strongest dominate. The weak become subservient. There's a pecking order. A hierarchy. And boy, it's not fun to be at the bottom. A lot of the time, the lowliest members don't make it. They're left behind or attacked by predators or sometimes killed by their own kind.

But Jesus marched bloodily to the top of a hill once, too, and what he did there looked much different. There, he chose invitation over intimidation, and he asks us to pick up our cross and climb the hill like him, not the gorilla. Because, despite being animals, we humans are also designed for the divine. There's a different Kingdom we're called to join. One that flips the animal kingdom on its head.

One where the strong take care of the weak. One where the first shall be last and the last shall be first. One, essentially, that's based not on primal instinct but on virtues that transcend our carnal urges.

Patience. Humility. Fortitude. Perseverance. Compassion.

In any other species, virtues like these would be a one-way ticket to extinction.

Somewhere—lodged in our most animalistic parts—we might hesitate to practice virtue for that very reason. We might think that by serving others before ourselves, we won't have what we need, and that would literally kill us.

But that's the animal in us talking.

Mary shows us that *with* virtue we not only survive, but find true, abundant life.

You see, Mary marched up the hill with Jesus, too. On that day and every other, she was brave enough to live for the divine—to live out virtue—with every breath she breathed. Not so *she* could be praised or glorified, mind you. She never shouts, "Look how great I am." Rather, her life boldly proclaims, "Look at the great I AM."

In essence, Mary became proof that, though we are animals, there is also something else—something divine—within us. Her life, then, is evidence of God's existence.

And by following her example, we can do that, too. Our very lives can be the picture of God's face, so long as we magnify him as Mary did.

That's why Mary is so important.

She knows what it takes to live like Christ, being courageous enough to stand out—and be set apart—for her Beloved in a world which did not know him. And though the world has changed drastically over the last two thousand years, the pursuit of holiness—and Holiness itself—remains the same.

In addition to being our example, Mary is also our constant companion and guide. Being the good Mother she is, she longs to slip her hand in ours as we attempt to navigate this broken world in a holy way. After all, Mary is not some fictional character from a story, but a real, living person who wants to interact with us and share an ongoing relationship.

So, with the help of God's grace and our loving Mother by our side, we can joyfully put others' needs before our own, even if it's an inconvenience to us. We can ponder, wrestle, and gnaw on the Truth. We can trust in God's plan, even if it takes a while to unfold or doesn't look the way we thought it would. We can uphold our word to others and resolutely accept our responsibilities. We can give our time, talents, and treasures to the Church and the people in our lives. We can choose courage in the face of fear. We can persevere through adversity and use our suffering as an offering on behalf of someone else. We can love people we disagree with and have compassion for those in need.

In short, we can be a tangible reminder of God in a world that has started to forget him. By doing so, we can live in a way that makes people squint and cock their head as though remembering a hazy dream—a dream that was placed deep in their hearts long ago. A dream of God.

We are called to live in a way that stirs and awakens the divinity in others.

We are called, each and every day, to live a real life that magnifies the Lord.

Acknowledgments

We are all made in the image and likeness of God—a God who is three Persons in One, a community in and of himself. Likewise, we are made to be in community with one another. For that, I am extremely grateful, for it's only through the friendships and examples in my life that I know what virtue looks like in action.

Dawn and Greg Luna—thank you for your unceasing generosity. First you gave me the gift of life. Then you've given me everything I could ever need to fill it with.

Mike and Kristine Gillespy—thank you for your charity and the humbling, self-sacrificial way you take care of my family and me. If not for you, I wouldn't be able to write a single word.

Jimmie Detraz—you are like a second mother to me. Thanks for taking on that responsibility and living it out so lovingly my whole life.

Exodus wives, Holy Spirit ladies, and DasCHE mommas—what on earth would I do without you? You all radiate virtue in your own unique ways and I, for one, consider myself lucky to witness the beauty you each bring to the world.

Stephanie Ridder—thanks for kicking my heinie into shape, physically and spiritually. Sheesh. Talk about toughness.

Sr. Allison Regina Gliot, Courtney Saponaro, and Sr. Orianne Pietra René Dyck—you all have no idea how filled up and inspired I am by your zeal. A mere editorial comment, phone call, or post on social media from you is enough to set my heart on fire for God. Thanks for letting me walk beside you on this journey of life and publishing.

Kyle, my best friend—thank you for showing me boundless amounts of patience and selflessness each day. You were the first to show me the face of Christ, and still to this day, you show me Jesus most clearly. Thank you for living out your faith in such a magnetic way and for leading our family with supernatural grace. You make it look easy. I'm just trying to keep up.

Marie, the girl who puts on her own shoes—someone once described you as the "definition of determination," and boy, that couldn't have been more spot on. God has given you superhuman amounts of perseverance. He must have done that knowing you'd have to put up with me every day.

Elizabeth—you are so young, and yet you've taught me almost everything I know about compassion. Thank you for using your big heart to care so beautifully for people, especially when they feel sad, hurt, or lonely.

John—your loyalty is fierce, my love. I'm so grateful you use it to shower me with such great love, and my heart melts when you pray that we will always be Jesus' friend.

Catherine—baby girl, from the moment you had words, you were using them to talk to Jesus. So, without even trying, you taught me what true prayerfulness looks like.

Philip—even before you were born, you were gifted with joy. It was so radiant, we watched you smile on two separate ultrasounds. Even the sonographer was stunned. I pray that you'll always and forever shock the world with your joy.

You, dear reader—thank you for your faith and contemplation. Without them, you'd never care to read this book.

Pauline
BOOKS & MEDIA

A mission of the Daughters of St. Paul

As apostles of Jesus Christ,
evangelizing today's world:

We are CALLED to holiness
by God's living Word and Eucharist.

We COMMUNICATE the Gospel message
through our lives and through all
available forms of media.

We SERVE the Church
by responding to the hopes and needs
of all people with the Word of God,
in the spirit of St. Paul.

For more information visit us at:
www.pauline.org